GW00600723

Rethinking Leaderhip

Rethinking Leadership

Kurt A. April
Graduate School of Business, University of Cape Town, South Africa

Robert Macdonald
ipac South Africa, Cape Town, South Africa

Sylvia Vriesendorp
Management Sciences for Health, Boston, MA, USA

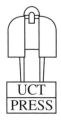

UCT
PRESS

First published 2000
Reprinted 2003
Reprinted December 2005
Reprinted December 2007
Reprinted February 2008

© University of Cape Town Press
PO Box 24309, Lansdowne 7779

This book is copyright under the Berne Convention. In terms of the Copyright Act 98 of 1978, no part of this book may be reproduced or transmitted in any form or by any means, (including photocopying, recording, or by any information storage and retrieval system) without permission in writing from the publisher.

ISBN 1-919-71353-0
ISBN 978-1-919-713-53-3

Typesetting and illustrations by Zebra Publications, Cape Town
Cover design by Gavin Younge
Printed and bound in South Africa by Creda Communications

About the authors

Kurt A. April

Kurt A. April, a Sainsbury Fellow and senior lecturer, lectures and researches in the disciplines of leadership and information management strategy at the Graduate School of Business of the University of Cape Town (South Africa). He lectures on the Master of Business Administration (MBA) programme, the Executive MBA programme, the Associate in Management (AIM) programme, as well as a number of executive short courses at the Business School. He was educated at the University of Cape Town, and obtained the following there: an MBA, a Masters degree in electronic engineering, a Bachelor's degree in electrical engineering, and a Higher Diploma in education; as well as two National Diplomas (electronic engineering; logic systems) at Wingfield College. He has also spent a year at Templeton College (Oxford University, UK) researching Information Management Strategy. Kurt has worked in a number of industries: defence (research engineer), rail transport (signals district engineer), nuclear power generation (process computing engineer), education (teacher of mathematics and physics), oil refining (instrumentation engineer). He has also consulted on various projects in the areas of knowledge management, information technology and leadership. Kurt has published a number of award-winning research papers in engineering journals, and co-authored a number of papers on the area of leadership with Robert Macdonald.

Since the early 1960s, the Graduate School of Business (GSB) of the University of Cape Town (UCT) has been a leader in providing world-class management education to top candidates, drawn locally and from abroad. Its international reputation and position as South Africa's leading business school is a status that has been earned — a reputation ultimately built on the success of its graduates. The school has a reputation for innovation in the face of changing circumstances, and is facing head-on the challenges of globalization within the South African economy, the turbulent business marketplace and multicultural challenges.

Robert Macdonald

Robert Macdonald is a former Director of the Master of Business Administration (MBA) programme at the Graduate School of Business of the University of Cape Town. He has convened various integrated business process courses at the Graduate School of Business and has focused much of his work on curriculum integration and project-based learning. Robert still teaches leadership on the MBA programme. Prior to joining the Graduate School of Business, Robert worked as a consultant in the field of economic and infrastructure development, and his current interests are in leadership development and management. Robert is now Head of Research and Investment Management at ipac South Africa, an investment company in Cape Town. Robert has Masters degrees in management studies and in modern history from Oxford University (UK), as well as a Masters degree in politics from Durham University (UK), and an undergraduate qualification in economics from the University of Cape Town. Robert has co-authored a number of papers on leadership with Kurt April.

ipac South Africa is a joint venture between South African financial services group Brait, and Australian financial planning and investment management group, ipac Securities Limited. ipac Securities, established in 1983, seeks to help individual investors and major financial institutions reach their financial goals reliably over time. ipac does this through a unique process of focusing on the needs of investors and developing investment strategies that cater specifically to their unique requirements. This process is based on rigorous research into financial products, fund managers and the economic environment.

Sylvia Vriesendorp

Sylvia Vriesendorp is a Senior Management Training and Organizational Development Specialist with Management Sciences for Health (MSH) in Boston, Massachusetts, USA. Her primary focus is to improve individual and organizational performance in public health programmes in developing countries. Before she joined MSH in 1986, Sylvia worked for the International Committee of the Red Cross in Lebanon, UNESCO's regional office in Senegal, and various US-based private voluntary agencies supporting family health programmes in developing countries. She designs and conducts management and leadership courses and workshops around the world and assists programmes and organizations in their strategic planning and organizational improvement efforts. She is the director of MSH's leadership courses in French and English, and frequently conducts training sessions for students in international public health at major US universities, including Boston University and Johns Hopkins University. Sylvia is the author of a book on strategic planning and has presented papers and conducted workshops at numerous professional conferences in the US and Africa. She is currently conducting research on leadership transitions in non-governmental organizations. She has a degree in psychology from the University of Leiden in the Netherlands.

Management Sciences for Health is a private, non-profit organization dedicated to closing the gap between what is known about public health problems and what is done to solve them. Through technical assistance, training, systems development, and applied research, MSH helps decision makers throughout the world use techniques of modern management to improve the delivery of health and family planning services. Management Sciences for Health collaborates with public- and private-sector counterparts in population, maternal and child health, information for management, drug management, health reform and financing, and management training. Since its founding in 1971, Management Sciences for Health has provided assistance in these areas to managers in over 100 countries. MSH's staff of 400 is based at its headquarters in Boston, two offices in Washington DC, and at many field offices throughout the world.

Acknowledgements

We would like to express our sincere and warm appreciation to several colleagues, friends and family, who read and prepared chapters, and gave input to the book. Their efforts, energy, passion, and love for the subject discipline made this book possible. In addition to our writings, chapters were prepared by:

- *Roger Breisch*. Management and Organizational Consultant, Partner of The Webber Group in Wheaton, USA and editor of *Entre Nous* (a publication of the Midwest Organizational Learning Network — MOLN, in Illinois, USA). Roger wrote the chapter: 'Followership — A Reflection on Leading by Following'.
- *Susan Hill*. Susan, a trained organizational and industrial psychologist, used to work in the human resources department of Shell (SA), but recently moved to Shell's new product development division, in which she plays a senior role. Susan wrote the chapter: 'Ambiguity — leadership incongruities, tensions and paradoxes'.

Special thanks to Colin Hall (executive chairman: Wooltru), Rory Wilson (CEO: Juta), Rosemary Shapiro (marketing director: NICRO), and Khanya Motshabi (chief operating officer: Future Growth) for their comments and insights into the topic of leadership, and their willingness to share, so freely, their experiences and understanding of people. Also, many thanks to Dr. Edward Gibson, an MBA graduate of the University of Cape Town, for sharing his passion and writings on servant-leadership. A very special thank you to our partners: Amanda (in Kurt's case), Helen (in Robert's case) and Axle (in Sylvia's case). Finally, we would like to thank everyone, including the MBA students at the Graduate School of Business of the University of Cape Town and our colleagues at UCT, ipac, and MSH, who have helped shape our ideas and thoughts, through conversation and dialogue, meetings, writings, and their enthusiasm for life. We especially appreciate the continued project commitment and the assistance that we have received from Glenda Younge, our publisher, and the staff at the University of Cape Town Press.

KURT A. APRIL
ROBERT MACDONALD
SYLVIA VRIESENDORP

Contents

Prologue
Leading in the New Millennium

My [countryfolk] are now called upon to move out of the physical plane of their journey and to carry it onto the mind and the spirit. They are now called upon to free
themselves from the Egypt of their worldly senses, from captivity in the Babylon of
their outer histories, and to carry the myth forward into a realm where race and physical being have no automatic privileged meaning. In such a realm kinship is determined
by the deeper and abiding considerations of life, for all those who, whatever their colour
of race, have answered the ancient challenge and have committed themselves to the
journey of becoming.

Van der Post, 1995

This book is a product of multiple authorship. In so being, it acknowledges the
complexity that characterizes leadership in the new millennium. It is no longer
sufficient to consider leadership as an individual pursuit. This notion belongs to
the increasingly outdated, yet in certain terrains still effective, concept of heroic
leadership. We believe that it is not possible to write something worthwhile about
leadership as an individual, because the perspective will be too limited. Hence this
book is written by a team made up of South Africans and Americans, a tribute to
the impact of modern technology and the Internet, but more importantly an
acknowledgement that these two countries, for very different reasons, are fascinating laboratories for studying leadership.

The United States of America has produced many of the leadership gurus,
including Peter Drucker, Warren Bennis, Tom Peters, Peter Senge, Stephen Covey
and many others. However, very little research has been carried out in this field in
South Africa, a country which experienced one form of leadership for most of the
twentieth century — autocratic control under the guise of apartheid. The social,
political, and economic freedom that now prevails in South Africa has provided for
the emergence of new leaders in all sectors of society. This has meant that a whole
range of new approaches to leadership is being experienced in business, government and civil society.

The fact that Americans and South Africans are writing a book about leadership is reflective of the globalization that is gripping the world. The concept of the
global village is gaining ground as we begin the twenty-first century. The 1998
World Competitiveness Report makes the link between South Africa and the US even
more interesting. The report ranks 46 countries according to their ability to cope
effectively with the process of internationalization. It examines, analyses and

ranks the ability of a nation to provide an environment that sustains the competitiveness of enterprises. Eight factors that impact on the extent to which the countries are achieving competitiveness are examined, namely: *government*, *infrastructure*, *management*, *research and development*, *people*, *finance*, the *domestic economy* and *internationalization* itself. The US comes out top of the scale in this evaluation, while South Africa languishes with Venezuela near the bottom of the table, only doing better than Russia, Poland and Colombia. In the category of *People* (where the main indicators are: the extent and attitude of the skilled labour force and quality of life) South Africa ranks last, as it has done for the past five years. Again, the US is at the other end of the scale.

The paradox of the US and South African contexts is that the realities of their economic situations contrast significantly with the experience of their respective national leaders. While South Africa is very much an emerging country with the challenge of climbing up the table of world competitiveness, it is a country that for much of the final decade of the twentieth century, provided the world with a universally acknowledged global leader in the person of Nelson Mandela. In 1999, while Mandela was being fêted across the world as a major moral and political leader, the President of the US, Bill Clinton — also a global leader by virtue of his position — was fighting for his political life as he became only the second US President to be impeached. Yet despite the contrasting fortunes of the US and South African political leaders, the US has moved into the twenty-first century in the best economic shape of its history, while South Africa makes the transition beset with economic problems, an unemployment rate of up to 40 % and a real GDP growth rate of well under 1 %.

Seventeenth-century scientific thinking would have us believe that leadership is a mechanical process — if certain requirements are met (for example, if the leader has certain qualities and the followers have a certain level of maturity) successful leadership will result. What then can we learn about leadership from the experiences of the US and SA at the start of the twenty-first century? Firstly, that leadership is not all that it seems to be. Perhaps the US and SA experiences highlight for us that success (however we wish to measure this) does not necessarily depend on the performance of the person at the top, that is, the leader. We realize of course, that leadership takes place at every level in society and every level of every sub-grouping thereof, organizations being the grouping in which most humans experience leadership. Hence, while Mandela speaks about reconciliation, the extent to which this has an impact on South Africa as a whole will depend hugely on the influence of the leadership that exists within the sub-groupings of South African society. Our seventeenth-century view of leadership would encourage us to see Mandela as the person with ultimate sway, but we are realizing more and more, as we enter the twenty-first century, that leadership is not only complex, but that it is more of a group process — a process of shared leadership. It may be argued that the success of the United States of America under Bill Clinton testifies to this understanding.

As a reader, your interest in this book is unique. Your reality is unique, and the interpretation you take away from this book is unique. This for us is the wonder of this concept called 'leadership'. We may wish that there was one 'right way' to be an effective leader, but certainly we have not been able to find that singular way in our work, nor in researching and writing for this book. Rather, we have identified a number of recurring themes in the area of leadership which we believe will be critical in the enactment of leadership in this new millennium. We believe that these themes are relevant to leaders no matter what the context, be it South Africa or the US or elsewhere, no matter the culture and no matter the people. It is always risky to declare 'universal truths', especially on a topic as complex as leadership. Nevertheless, we believe that, if leaders are aware of the themes that we have identified and take this awareness into their lives, especially their personal lives, their effectiveness as leaders will be greatly enhanced.

Unsurprisingly, the first theme we have identified is that of *awareness*. As a leader it is, and will be, critical to be aware on a number of fronts, not only of yourself, but of others as well as of the context in which you operate. As a way of developing this awareness, we offer four metaskills to assist in this process.

The first metaskill deals with an *awareness of paradox* and that there may be a need to let go of having always to be certain of choices and outcomes. This is becoming less possible in our complex world. In order to cope, we are faced with the urgency to do more, quickly, while at the same time needing to reflect ('being') in order for our 'doing' to be more effective.

In order to operate more effectively in this world of paradox, we suggest that the second metaskill you require is that of *knowing yourself*. You need to understand from which mental models you operate, how you respond in certain situations, what assumptions you and others make. We introduce the notion of 'self-doubt' as a quality which is an inherent part of knowing yourself.

We see the third important metaskill as *knowing where you want to go*, or where you think you want to go.

The fourth and final metaskill which we highlight is that of *understanding power and group dynamics*. A key to this skill is self-awareness, because we look at how group dynamics operate at a primary (or work-group) level, as well as at a secondary (or basic assumptions) level, where much that happens is below the surface. Without self-awareness, we are unable to tap into the secondary processes that are happening all around us, but which are not necessarily obvious to us on a surface level.

Awareness is the theme that underpins and is critical to *all* that leadership is about. *Awareness* of self and others is the starting point, we believe, of effective leadership.

As we begin this new millennium we need to be open to change. This openness means that we need be prepared to rethink the way we view the world, and be prepared to change our perceptions and the habits that we have built up over time. In chapter 2, we examine *openness* and consider the age-old debate of management versus leadership, and through this debate encourage leaders to be open to other points of view, rather than assuming that it is critical to have the right or the wrong stance. Leadership theory has changed over time, and if we are not open to moving with the developments in such thought, it is likely that we, as leaders, will be stuck in old ways of doing things.

Although we have already stated that the move into the new millennium is one that will be characterized by *complexity,* (a topic which we explore in chapter 4), there will be the paradoxical need for leaders to seek simplicity in all that they do. In chapter 3 we consider how this *simplicity* might be achieved by looking at the insights that the new sciences are offering us. Much of present-day thinking about leadership is based on seventeenth-century Newtonian thinking, which tends to reinforce the mechanical, top-down view of leadership. Quantum physics (part of the new sciences) tells us that relationships are building blocks of life in the natural world, and this suggests to us that our human existence is no different. We see through the new sciences a confluence with traditional African philosophy, in which the notion of *Ubuntu* informs us that we exist as people only in relationship with others. The Newtonian view of the world told us to break things down into parts; the new sciences are telling us to build relationships, view things as wholes not parts, and seek simplicity in leading by focusing on certain core issues. In dealing with *complexity,* as discussed in chapter 4, we often do try to simplify and make our lives easier and more certain. However, what we learn from chaos theory is that we can no longer seek to be in control of everything; we can no longer afford to seek out certainty as quickly as possible, for the impact of these approaches will force us into simplistic solutions that do not acknowledge the systemic complexity of the world in which we live. The paradoxes for a long time have been hidden behind rational, mechanical models that supposedly provide the answers and create certainty and therefore predictability. The new sciences tell us to live, and be comfortable with, uncertainty; to allow chaos to unfold and not strive for control. The natural world is showing us that life is about process, not outcomes — a perspective that African and Eastern cultures have held for centuries; a perspective that we believe is critical for leadership in this new millennium.

The focus on process rather than on outcomes is explored in chapter 5, where we consider the critical concept of *connectivity* in a world of relationships. This follows through to the idea that strategy is a *process,* not a concrete plan — a perspective we discuss in chapter 6. In terms of *connectivity,* the key skill that leaders are going to need to master is that of communication, and in this regard we focus specifically on the process of dialogue; a process of conversing in which all those involved concentrate on creating new meaning, rather than on getting across personal points of view. This skill and process can then be taken into the realm of strategy development, which, since time immemorial, has been seen as the domain of the leader.

That strategy can no longer be seen as the sole responsibility of the leader takes us into chapter 7 and the paradoxical reminder that leadership is as much about

Followership as it is about leading. This concept is closely linked to that of *steward-ship*, which we look at in chapter 8, where we see the leader as a servant of those who follow, and a steward of whatever entity or organization is being led.

Both the concepts of *followership* and *stewardship* are helpful to leaders who need to harness the increasingly common reality of diversity. Diversity is not explored in a standalone chapter, but the issue of diversity reminds the leader that, if he or she acts as a follower or a servant to the needs of followers, a rich variety of talent, experience and world-view is there to be harnessed. The global village is forcing leaders from all corners of the world to confront and deal with this issue of diversity, but it is critical to see diversity as integral to all the themes in this book.

This new millennium will be a time of less certainty than before. Global markets at times will seem fickle, job security will be fleeting — change is the only global reality. In this environment of turbulence, we believe that the themes of this book will serve as sources of solidity; beacons to hang onto when catching your breath. Chapter 9 explores possibly the most important one of these themes, that of *ambiguity*, as it reviews all the incongruities and paradoxes so inherent in the leadership process.

Being comfortable with *ambiguity* will probably be the greatest challenge that leaders will face throughout this new millennium. We believe, however, that an effective level of comfort can be achieved through *awareness* of self and others; *openness* to change and new ideas; a genuine striving for *simplicity* in a world of growing *complexity*, through a focus on *connectivity* and *process*, rather than an obsession with outcome, while remaining mindful at all times of the benefits of *followership*, *diversity* and *stewardship*, each of which can be ignored in the short term but is critical for sustainable leadership. The need for sustainable leadership can only come through a *consciousness* which acknowledges that our human experience is beyond the material. We believe firmly that an *awareness* of these themes, a genuine attempt to integrate them into our lives, and an acceptance of the *ambiguity* that underpins any form of leadership, will be the only recipe for successfully leading in the new millennium.

Awareness
The Metaskills of the Leader

Highly effective people have learned to integrate a localized focus with comprehensive awareness. They zero in on the present moment without losing the broader sense of their vision and purpose. Being deeply focused yet simultaneously aware of the meaningful context of our lives is one of the keys to inside-out success.

Cashman, 1998

While leaders and managers in Brazil, Burkina Faso, South Africa and Bangladesh are trying to find quick fixes to intractable problems through re-engineering, total quality management (TQM), a focus on productivity, action and results, leaders in the West, and in particular the United States, are taking stock, taking a deep breath, and coming to the conclusion that this life is killing us. And it literally is. According the 1998 *World Health Report* issued by the World Health Organization (WHO), circulatory diseases account for 46 % of total deaths in the developed world. Stress-related diseases such as coronary heart disease, stroke and mental disorders are on the rise in developing countries, with circulatory diseases accounting for one quarter of all deaths in developing countries during the period 1985–1997 (WHO, 1998). In fact, cardiovascular disease and other lifestyle-related non-communicable diseases are increasing much faster now in the developing countries than earlier last century in the industrialized countries (Martin, 1997: 5).

The illusion of control

What is killing us is the illusion of control: that things can be predictable, consistent and forever under control. What is also killing us is that followers require their leaders to be in control, on top of things, and to take the blame when things go wrong. To a certain extent, we have come to expect perfection from our leaders. Much of the management literature over the last few decades has focused on how to analyse and control other people and circumstances, either directly or through carefully designed systems. Nearly all the new management programmes on TQM, re-engineering, right-sizing, just-in-time, this or that, are really old wine in new bottles — more efforts to design control systems that ask the workers to try harder; do better and be even more productive. And much of the popular press and the media are on a continuous search for leaders who are responsible for the messes we have found ourselves in.

Being in control — and having all the answers — is something that is rooted in our earliest life experiences. According to Chris Argyris (1990), being in control is particularly important when we deal with situations that are threatening or embarrassing. Out of our earliest experiences with these situations we develop our 'theories of action', programs in our heads, like software, that regulate how we deal with future threatening or embarrassing situations. This software tells us to be in unilateral control, to win and not to upset people. Our strategies are to persuade and sell, and save our own and other people's face. If this theory-in-use (the actual rules we use to manage our beliefs) is indeed as universal as Argyris and his colleagues (Argyris and Schön, 1978, Argyris, 1982; 1985) claim, then we can understand why the need to control remains firmly in control. And while the new leader is trying to get the situation under control (dealing with all the problems left by a predecessor), and putting all the ideals and the vision temporarily in the refrigerator (until things are under control of course!), there is the surprise of what Warren Bennis calls his First Law of (Academic) Pseudo-dynamics: 'routine work drives out non-routine work [that is, pursuing the vision and the plans for fundamental change] and smothers to death all creative planning, all fundamental change in the university — or any institution' (Bennis 1993b: 73). And before the leader realizes what is happening to him- or herself, he or she is in a permanent coping mode, reacting to the environment and its innumerable and conflicting demands, dodging accusations of incompetence, slowly drowning in paperwork, in reports, endless meetings, negotiations and requests. The leader's increasingly tired, defensive and irritable reactions set conditions and a tone for leadership that can hardly be called fulfilling to the self, or inspiring to others. The leader's coping and reactive mode are unlikely to provide him or her with a sense of safety, security or self-confidence.

A new set of skills

A new set of skills is needed. These are not the usual skills taught to leaders or aspiring leaders in executive courses on such topics as time management, delegation, writing, public speaking, conflict resolution, negotiation, and the like. This is a different set of skills, for which a new word has been coined: *metaskills*. *Metacognition* can be defined as an individual's awareness of of his or her own cognitive processes, and his or her ability to control these processes by organizing, monitoring, and modifying them as a function of environmental factors (Silver, 1993). Thus, metaskills are the skills that we need to bring about this awareness. Metaskills are the skills that we need to examine ourselves, the secondary processes, the irrational or subconscious processes that influence our feelings and behaviour, and our connections to each other and the rest of the universe. We apply metaskills when we consciously examine the unspoken conversations that go on in our minds. According to Arnold and Amy Mindell, two American psychologists, the development of metaskills allows us to go beyond mere coping with our environment and reacting to it, to a point where we have 'a feeling sense' and something called the 'second' attention, a term used by Carlos Castaneda's teacher Don Juan, which refers to an enduring and heightened sense of awareness: 'One can feel with the eyes, when the eyes are not looking right into things' (Brockman, 1998). Thus, for the purposes of this chapter, we will define the metaskills of a leader as the *skills needed to step back and look at ourselves in our broader contexts (family, work, community, the world, the universe) in order to raise our awareness, consciousness and understanding of who we are, why we are here, how we operate and how that affects others and our environment.*

Metaskills are not that tangible or easy to recognize. Margaret Wheatley (1992; 1999) talks about walking with soft eyes, that is, seeing what's around us without focusing on any particular spot. Chris Argyris (1990; 1994) talks about left and right columns, an imagined or real dialogue written up on the left side of the page, with the unsaid or undiscussable thoughts or feelings on the right side. The right side brings to awareness all that we do not express, because we feel we cannot be truthful and say what we really mean. The work of Argyris influenced much of Senge's (1990b) thinking about learning organizations and the role of our mental models — the basic, 'sacred' assumptions we hold about work, about people, about life, about the universe — and how we work these assumptions, unexamined, into our reasoning, which ultimately determines our action.

Since the development of metaskills is primarily about increasing awareness, we will explore four areas in which increased awareness may serve us well:

1. Awareness of paradoxes
2. Awareness of self and others
3. Awareness of our vision
4. Awareness of power and group dynamics

This is a good time to work on developing metaskills. The leadership and management market is imbued with a new vocabulary: chaos, fluidity, flexibility, stewardship, empowerment, self-knowledge, spirituality, guiding values. The messages are remarkably similar, and many have their roots in deeply held spiritual values and practices that have been around for ages. The ancient wisdom of the world has survived in the forms of stories, myths and legends, fairy tales, sacred books and scrolls. It is enjoying a renewed popularity, if judged by the ever-expanding shelves in large bookstores dedicated to these texts, and the placement of books about spirituality in the business and management section. This 'new' old wisdom has been allowed into the corporate boardroom, and is the latest in a series of American-dominated exports to the business community around the world. It is ironic, and sad, that the West and the North are now exporting, back to the world, the paradigms they have rooted out with so much zeal in their old colonies. Some Native American elders say that traditional knowledge is never lost, and cannot be rooted out, because it exists independent from people, as spirits or energies. Peat (1994: 68) tells the story of a (Native American) man who went to a ceremony and could not get a particular song out of his head. When encouraged to sing it out aloud by one of the elders, it was recognized as Joe's song. Joe had died in 1910. That the song had come back did not surprise the elders, ' . . . it got kind of lonely waiting around with no one to sing it'. This 'return to the roots' is encouraging. The realization by the Western, so-called developed countries, that everything in the universe is inter-connected, and that the splits between work and family, body and soul, animate and inanimate world, men and women, animals and people are all artificial, will do much to heal the rifts that this fragmentation has brought about.

The resurgence of the old wisdom, the yearning for connections (to the spirit, to each other, to the earth) is an expression of the profound sense of alienation that the Western corporate world has created among its workers, and in particular the age group that came into leadership positions during the last twenty years. As Joseph Jaworski, creator of the American Leadership Forum, describes in his book *Synchronicity:* 'Mine was a Disney World sort of life — unauthentic, narrow, utterly predictable, and largely devoid of meaning' (Jaworski, 1996: 31). The irony is that, by traditional American standards, he had achieved the pinnacle of success!

Metaskill 1: Exploring the paradoxes

Since Descartes made a pact with the Pope to split the human experience in two, and split the mind and spirit from the body, we have wandered into a place that keeps presenting us with paradoxes that we think we have to resolve somehow. Things are either white or black, mind or matter, so we are constantly confronted with these paradoxes that create great tensions in our lives. Our habitual response to resolving them has been to deny one side or the other, depending whether we feel more aligned with the university or the church.

Success sucks

When at the pinnacle of (economic or academic) success, the feeling so often is one of *not* being successful, of being a cheat. Will Schutz, an early architect of Esalen (an educational centre devoted to the exploration of unrealized human capacities, founded in 1962 on the California coast near Big Sur) describes the same feeling Jaworski mentioned: 'The next few years continued to be outwardly quite successful, but something was wrong. I was straining at the edges of traditional techniques. Although I loved the classroom and the teaching process, I never felt fully adequate. I felt phony. I assigned classes the second-best book in the field while I read ahead in the best book and lectured from it. I did not feel I *knew* anything from my own experience' (Schutz, 1994: 3). This is not a new phenomenon. In her best-selling book, *The Cinderella Complex*, first published nearly two decades ago, Collette Dowling described successful women's tendency to ascribe their success not to their own ability but to magic or some force outside themselves. The conclusion is that one must therefore be a cheat! The ongoing conversation about the redefinition of what is success, and what is truly important in life is putting to rest this paradox of unhappily chasing economic success in the name of happiness. This was never really a paradox, but rather a predictable outcome of a long series of life choices and practices.

Boring balance and the thrill of turbulence

Another paradox is the search for balance, order and harmony in life, and the new knowledge that equilibrium is not what we should be pursuing, because equilibrium equals death (Burgess quoted in Kelly, 1994: 92). Equilibrium and order, or the absence of stimulation and stresses, are not the conditions for optimal growth and development in the natural world. The pursuit of order is an illusion, and the assumption that order will make our lives more bearable, less stressful and thus healthier, only works (if it works at all) for those who benefit from the order (usually those on the top of the societal, political or organizational pyramid) and then only for a while (after which success sucks). Because, in the end, order and equilibrium may solve some problems, but create others. Silas Katana, a farmer in Kilifi district in Kenya, has a particular view on order in his fields: 'It is always the same when I plant in straight lines, if there are mice, they start eating at one end and move on swiftly straight down the line, and I quickly lose the whole crop. I always replant randomly, because there is a greater chance that less seeds will be found by the mice this way' (quoted in Chambers, 1997: 162).

We have learned much about and from large ecosystems. Experiments undertaken to replicate particular landscapes, deserts, rainforests, have taught us that it is turbulence, being *out of equilibrium*, which makes the system robust, and which makes for growth and strength. Turbulence and disorder is, as the inhabitants of Biosphere 2 (a gigantic glass ark, sealed from the outside world, simulating a closed vivisystem) discovered, the incredible subsidy we receive from nature. In the well-controlled domed biosphere environment, without nature's turbulence and its chaotic unpredictability, the inhabitants of Biosphere 2 spent hours per day weeding (controlling) plants that outgrew their allocated spaces. In nature the forest fires, the rainstorms, falling trees and hurricanes — unpredictable, chaotic, turbulent — upset the balance and thus allow for renewal and growth through periodical recycling of nutrients, and thus do the work for us (Kelly, 1994: 152). Of course we know this already, on a deeper level, from personal experience. When are the times of our biggest personal growth? When did we learn the most significant things? Usually we can trace these occurrences back to times of turbulence in our lives, and learning was usually accompanied by periods of significant physical or psychological discomfort. If our job as leaders is to allow for renewal and growth, for the recycling of nutrients in our workplaces, for creativity and new approaches to old problems (which may well have been the promise through which we were elected or appointed) then had we better brace ourselves for chaos, uncertainty and turbulence. How?

The organizational equivalent of turbulence and disorder is often mistaken for anarchy and chaos, and thus deemed highly undesirable. Organizational order is maintained at all cost. Here too is the illusion of control. But we pay a price which isn't immediately obvious: order and control spawn dependency, complacency. They kill initiative, inventiveness, resourcefulness, and creativity. They depress morale and take the joy out of work and living. Joel Henning, in his foreword to Peter Block's book *Stewardship*, likens American corporations to authoritarian religious organizations, governed by three basic principles: compliance, watching (checking on compliance), and trying harder in the face of breakdown or failure (Block, 1993: xiv). None of this does much for the human spirit. So, in the belief of improving clarity, we fine-tune job descriptions, establish lines of control and tell people exactly what we want. All this to avoid chaos (meaning turbulence). Letting go is hard, because we may not be able to predict what we get, a great worry of many leaders. As Kevin Kelly observed, looking at the many ways in which scientists tried to manipulate ecosystems, 'It was very easy to arrive at a stable ecosystem, if you didn't care what system you arrived at' (Kelly, 1994: 63). The challenge for the leader is that he or she *does* care where we end up. So the challenge for leaders is to hold this paradox: letting go of the actual architecture of the result without letting go of what we really care about, the values, the vision that undergird the result. The paradox is also maintaining the equilibrium while embracing the creative power of turbulence. There is a children's toy, called *duikelaar* in Dutch. It is a plastic clown with a weighted bottom. No matter how it falls, it is always able to right itself, swinging wildly back and forth for a moment, but always coming to rest, centred on its weighted core. That is what we are after!

From nouns to verbs and from acting to being

We are turning what used to be static objects (nouns) into dynamic actions (verbs). Things of 'being' are turned into things of 'doing'. Many of our body parts have become verbs: eyeing, nosing, shouldering, elbowing, mouthing, heading, backing, fingering, toeing. The state of 'being in dialogue' has become a verb: dialoguing, and has triggered the development of a whole new professional species: the dialogue consultant. In America, *doing* something is highly valued. The no-nonsense manager acts, is decisive. The one who sits quietly and reflects on life is not really working. 'Off with your head' the Queen of Hearts would say.

Never have the East and West clashed more profoundly than on the dimension of 'being' versus 'doing'. The Western business breakfast, its fast-food and fast-everything culture, stands in sharp contrast to the meditative practices from the East. 'Don't just sit there, do something', is a familiar phrase in the US, and unfortunately also in the upper echelons of organizations around the world. Spending time with one's staff, reflecting on where the organization has come from and where it is heading, is still too often considered something 'we have no time for'. No wonder work is called busy-ness! And now, even the airlines encourage those flying in business class to remain busy: computers can be connected and even recharged, phone and fax lines are provided to communicate with the office thousands of miles away, on the ground. Busy-ness is a badge of honour, piles of paper on one's desk a sign of importance. The example is set for the next generation entering the workplace. And this next generation is well prepared: in the US parents have also been telling *kids* to not just sit there, but do something! Some children have such tight schedules of classes and lessons that they are chronically stressed out. They are being cheated out of their childhood because their parents fear that their children would miss the boat (towards 'success') if they would be lounging around, and just be.

At an organizational level, all this individual action adds up to a lot of energy, exhaustion, and eventually bad tempers and irritations. The sad dynamic of all of these spinning wheels is that many of the efforts cancel each other out and raise the general level of frustration and despair, with no time just to sit and talk things over, or to step back and take the long view. The consequence of our busy-ness has been serious, both on a personal and a global level. No one has time to reflect on long-term impact, or to explore what certain interventions really are about. So-called development projects have uprooted whole villages and increased the rich–poor gap. Careless use and disposal of resources have created intractable problems for future generations. The US departments of Energy and of Environmental Protection are struggling to clean up countless messes left behind by factories and defence projects that neglected to think about the impact of their methods of waste disposal in the middle of this century.

We are beginning to discover this. At an intuitive level most of us know that in times of extreme motion and flux (an avalanche, a maelstrom, a strong wind or current), our chances of survival increase if we stop thrashing, trying to swim, and come up for air. At work we are discovering that in planning exercises it is no longer the planning of the Plan that counts, because we have learned that the Plan will be outdated before the year is over. We have come to see that it is the process of planning, the *being* together, that is the result that we want: finding out what the world looks like from someone else's vantage point; finding out how an action will impact on people seven generations from now. Increasingly, strategic planning exercises are no longer about creating the Plan. Rather, the most important thing becomes the act of engaging in conversation and dialogue with others and creating the vision. The formation of the Club of Rome in 1968 was a first loud wake-up call to the West for what we were doing on a global level (Meadows, Meadows, Randers and Behrens, 1972). Heart attacks, suicides and broken marriages were the wake-up calls at a personal level. The paradox is that we need to act so we can be.

Mending the splits

We can no longer ignore the damaging effects of splitting our world into opposites. We have to stop making a distinction between 'doing' as work and 'being' as non-work, splitting family from work as if the two are unrelated, and realize that the professional and personal are closely connected. 'Corporate poet' David Whyte points out that, sooner or later, we realize that we shortchange ourselves by 'removing portions of our life from exploration, as if, at work, certain parts of experience suddenly lie out of bounds'. Whyte continues: 'Life does not seem to be impressed by our arguments that we can ignore our deeper desires simply because we happen to be earning a living at the time' (Whyte, 1994: 69).

Taking time out for quiet reflection

In sports, when the coach makes a T-sign with his two hands, it means time out, a time to stop the game temporarily and huddle together, to talk strategy and get a take on how each player is feeling about the game thus far. In business we should do the same — think about the long-term consequences of this move, or, as Native Americans say, think about the impact of this move on the seventh generation coming after us. Taking time out for ourselves is more difficult. It means taking our vacations rather than letting the days accumulate. It means writing in a journal on a regular basis. Or going for long walks, alone or with people who are important to us. Or meditating, participating in religious ceremonies, reading the world's masterpieces, listening to music, listening to our own heartbeat and learning to read the signals our bodies send to us to indicate that we are agitated, or sad, or angry . . . and need to take time out — what Stephen Covey terms 'Quadrant III stuff'. Lao Tsu admonishes us to unclutter our minds and develop the quality of our consciousness by letting go of all the new theories and techniques, and giving up trying to know all the time just what to do (Heider, 1986: 95). Instead, when we stop trying so hard, and accept that we do not know what to do, and sit still and listen, we will find all that we need to know in the silence.

The Quakers (a Christian religion founded by George Fox in 1652 in England, in reaction to the heavily regulated, bureaucratized and institutionalized form that religious practices had taken at the time) worship in silence. Fox felt that ordinary man had gotten too far removed from God. In the silence, the gathered congregation waits for the Lord, who may speak through anyone present. It is thus a very egalitarian religion, with no priests or intermediaries who act on behalf of God. The *being* becomes easier. If one cannot sit still for one hour and listen in silence, one will thus not receive any illumination. Similarly, our intuition is of no use if we do not listen to what it has to say. But the moment we withdraw from the visual and aural clutter around us, by closing our eyes, by praying, by walking in the woods, or, for some, by dreaming, we will find all that we need at our disposal. This is how we become mindful, able to take in the details of life around us: a sight, a facial expression, but also the wonders of nature, the wisdom of animals and the creative powers of the universe. Only if we slow down and take time out can we find the time to increase our awareness of ourselves, where we come from, where we are heading and how we impact on the people around us. A mindful walk in the woods is a walk 'with soft eyes', as Wheatley calls it, a walk during which we take in everything without focusing on any one thing. After practising in the woods, try a walk across the factory floor or the open-plan office, in the maternity ward, through the office — with soft eyes!

Metaskill 2: Knowing oneself and the other

We behave the way we do for good reasons: those behaviours have usually served us well in the past. Our tendency to include or exclude ourselves in groups, to want to lead others or want to be led, and our longing for intimacy or just the opposite has grown out of adaptive responses that made sense in our past (Schutz, 1994). But how rigidly do we adhere to these tendencies? Can we adapt our behaviour to different circumstances, the requirements of the situation? Or have we become rigid in our ways? Old tapes are being replayed, these are often 'parent-tapes,' voices of authority, when we find ourselves in situations that have some resemblance to something in our past. And when we react as the little child did years ago, we will not be very effective.

Finding out who we are, where we have come from, and why we are here, can give us some answers to these questions. If we are busy, doing things, we have no time to ask these existential questions. But if we journal or walk in the woods we can. Painful moments are good times to learn. Why did I react so strongly to this person? Why did I raise my voice? Why did my palms sweat? Of course you have to notice these things before you can reflect on them. The focus of our energy on others needs to be redirected to ourselves. Instead of 'why did she behave so aggressively?' I should be asking: 'What was it about her aggressive behaviour that triggered something in me?' 'Who does she remind me of?' 'Where has this happened before?' and 'How often is this happening to me?'

Who am I?

Leadership implies the exercise of power and authority. How we relate to these two often has its roots in what we observed around us and how we were told to relate to them when we were little. Nelson Mandela, in his autobiography, describes how his earliest experiences with power and authority shaped his notions about leadership: the tribal meetings at the Great Place, at Mqhekezweni in what is now called Eastern Cape, where the regent listened to any and all who came to speak to him, often with grievances and criticism. He remembers his astonishment at the vehemence and candid ways in which the leader was criticized, and, more importantly, he remembered how the regent simply listened, without defending himself, showing no emotion at all. 'As a leader, I have always followed the principles I first saw demonstrated by the regent at the Great Place. I have always endeavoured to listen to what each and every person in a discussion had to say before venturing my own opinion' (Mandela, 1996: 25).

Whether positive, as in Mandela's case, or negative (an abusive parent or other authority figure), early childhood experiences shape much of our adult behaviour. Kets de Vries, a psychoanalyst and Professor of Human Resource Management at INSEAD in France, has married the disciplines of psychoanalytic theory and organization theory, exploring the role of unconscious motivation in explaining human action and decision making in organizations. Laurent Lapierre (in Kets de Vries, 1991), a founding member of the International Society for the Psychoanalytic Study of Organizations, emphasizes the unconscious and irrational aspects of leadership by adopting the following definition of leadership: 'Leadership is that part of executive action that may be directly attributed to the inner life of the leader, to her personal vision, her ways of being and acting, her deep-rooted beliefs, her imagination, and her fantasies' (Lapierre in Kets de Vries, 1991: 70). Thus, according to Kets de Vries, it is important for leaders to realize how power, or the exercise of leadership itself, ' . . . can activate, or re-activate the most primitive and archaic fantasies that lie at the core of intellectual activity and individual behaviour' (1991: 72).

How to understand oneself and discover these primal fantasies that guide our behaviour has been an age-old pursuit. This, according to some, is why we have myths and legends. From the ancient myths to today's storytellers, the messages are remarkably similar, no matter where one is in the world. There is a re-emergence of interest in fables and myths as a way to go 'inside' and understand those primal fantasies that are at the root of our behaviour. Jung (see Storr, 1983), Campbell (1949), Pearson (1989), Pinkola Estes (1992) and Whyte (1994) have used myths, legends and archetypes to help us make the journey inward, and understand the dynamic forces that shape who we are and how we handle the exercise of power. Whether we understand where our beliefs or assumptions come from or not, we may simply reflect on how we use them and whether they serve us well or not.

The term 'mental models', the theories that most of us have about the nature of the situations around us, was used by Jay Forrester, who developed the concepts and applications of system dynamics in the mid 1950s when he was at the Massachusetts Institute of Technology (MIT) in the United States helping manufacturers deal with the fluctuations in orders and production capacity (Kleiner, 1996: 207). Art Kleiner (1996), in his fascinating account of the 'story of management' in the US since World War II, describes the various streams of intellectual influences and emotionally charged controversies that have shaped managerial culture. Both the overall story and the individual accounts show how mental models have both helped and hindered the growth and expansion of major corporations that currently dominate the world scene. At an individual level, mental models help us navigate the complex world. These models develop over time, shaping what Chris Argyris (1990: 88) calls the 'ladder of inference'. Essentially, the ladder of inference is based on a theory of action — a conclusion to do or say (or not do or not say) something based on inferences derived from cultural meanings ascribed to directly observable data, such as a conversation or verbal cues. Rick Ross (in Senge, Kleiner, Roberts, Ross and Smith, 1995: 242) simplified the ladder and added two rungs to it: as I observe something, I quickly run up the steps in my mind; I select certain data from all that happens around me; I add meaning to this subset of data; I make assumptions based on the meaning I added; I draw conclusions which then inform my action. Thus we believe that:

> What we think is the truth
> The truth is obvious
> Our beliefs are based on objective and solid data
> The data we selected are the only data.

> *Ross (in Senge et al., 1995: 242)*

In a variation on this theme Bolman and Deal (1991) refer to the 'mystery–mastery' model of interpersonal behaviour. In this model, a series of steps is followed to reason oneself out of a problem situation by assuming that the problem is caused by the other person(s), which leads to a unilateral diagnosis and a solution that requires the other to change. We will try to do this by arguing the merits of our solution; by asking leading questions to manipulate the other; and by telling the other directly what he or she is doing wrong and how he or she should change. If the other person resists or becomes defensive, our original diagnosis is thus confirmed. We then step up the pressure and if our efforts are unsuccessful, or less successful than hoped, it is the other's fault (1991: 137). This chain of reasoning is rampant and at the root of many so-called interpersonal problems in organizations that have led to transfers and firing of people, and thus to much suffering and despair. Unfortunately, many of these mental models are untested and unexamined.

Although we may think that they have served us well, they actually have not, and have gotten us into much trouble which we may always have attributed to other people and forces outside ourselves as the reasoning above illustrates. The challenge is to examine them. Three sets of skills will help us with that: *introspection* (rather than accusing others, examine how we ourselves may have contributed to a problem or situation), *reflection* (stepping back and slowing down our thinking processes to become more aware) and *inquiry* (asking questions to test our assumptions). These skills will allow us to re-script the doomed reasoning and take us to a better place. Instead of looking for a place to put blame, we agree on the basics (the task, the process); we search for common ground; we experiment; we doubt our own infallibility, and we treat differences as a group responsibility.

At an organizational level, if the mental models and the essential beliefs of the leader are being imposed onto the entire organization, we will see the beliefs translated into structures. For example, Banner and Gagné (1995: 92) list a number of such beliefs and the corresponding organizational structures, such as 'people can't be trusted to do the right thing organizationally', which necessitates strong formalization, close supervision and centralization. Kets de Vries and Miller (1987: 110) describe a number of 'neurotic' organizational types and the corresponding executive behaviours, culture, strategy and guiding themes, illustrating the same principle. Gareth Morgan, in his book *Images of Organization* (1986), presents and explores the idea that our theories and explanations of organizational life are based on metaphors that create special filters through which we see and come to understand organizations. Knowing whether we see the organization as an organism, a machine, a psychic prison, a culture, a political system, as a system in constant flux and transformation, or as a tool of domination, will help us better understand why we pursue certain strategies, put in place certain structures and deal with organizational problems in certain ways (Morgan, 1986). McGregor, in his now classic 1960 book *The Human Side of Enterprise*, suggests a simple exercise to explore the assumptions, generalizations and hypotheses people hold about organizations. (As a variant, try to apply this to yourself.)

> Next time you attend a staff meeting at which a policy issue is under discussion or some action is being considered, try a variant on the pastime of doodling. Jot down the assumptions, beliefs, opinions, convictions, generalizations about human behavior made during the discussion by the participants. Some of these will be explicitly stated . . . Most will be implicit but fairly easily inferred . . . It will not make much difference whether the problem is human, financial or technical.

> *McGregor, 1960: 6*

Others who are different

In a dramatic story about the clash of two cultures in a Californian town, the US world of medical science and the immigrant (refugee) Hmong culture crashed head-on and many people got hurt. The outward 'adaptation' of the Hmong to the US culture deceived the American doctors into thinking that they could and should be treated like everyone else, and that interpreters or speaking slower English would be enough to bridge the gap. Aside from a description of the manifesting symptoms, few caretakers thought about asking the Hmong patients what they thought caused their suffering. And if they did, the stories about spirits were discounted as useless for deciding on a treatment plan. According to one doctor:

> If you went down to the rain forest and talked to the [local tribal people] you'd be surprised if they *didn't* come up with all sorts of fantastic spirit stories. You'd be surprised if they sat there and started saying, you know, 'Where's the penicillin for my impetigo?' But if you took them to this [Californian] setting and dressed them up and they drove a car and came to [the hospital], you wouldn't expect to hear those stories anymore.

> *Fadiman, 1997: 112*

This misunderstanding had disastrous consequences for many people involved and caused a lot of suffering that could have been avoided, if only the people involved had realized that no one has a hold on the truth, or, as one social worker remarked, 'our view on reality is only a view, not reality itself (Fadiman, 1997: 276).

Ronnie Lessem (1996) describes the four paradigms that come together in South Africa (and not only here) in his book *From Hunter to Rainmaker: The Southern African Businessphere*, the East, the West, the North, the South each have their own ways of looking at and interpreting the world. Each one of us acts out of one paradigm or another, and this determines what we look at, what we consider significant, how we see cause and effect, and thus how we act. As the world is coming together through technology and wars, the paradigms bump into each other, as they did in the Health Centre in California, and create even more turbulence. It is unavoidable. Whether we like it or not, we *have to* take off our glasses, step aside, and look through the other's windows. In his critique of the predominant paternalistic North–South development paradigm, *Whose Reality Counts: Putting the First Last*, Robert Chambers invites the Northerners and Westerners to open up to self-doubt. 'Self-doubt implies that others may know or may be right. Understanding that realities are multiple, and that other's realities differ from one's own and from each other, this becomes a way forward, a means of learning and doing better' (Chambers, 1997: 203). Thus the task of the expert becomes one of listening and unlearning, from being the knower to becoming the sharer and learner, and not just in the area of soft and fuzzy wisdom, but also when it comes to what the Western World often considers 'hard' knowledge, the nuts and bolts (like medicine, demography . . .) (Marindo-Ranganai quoted in Chambers, 1997: 231).

The political mindset, which assumes that resources are limited and that some people will win and others will lose, has been a powerful force in our interactions with each other and created, especially in the Western World, a strong sense of competition for resources and for recognition. We are constantly exposed to zero-sum competition around us: races, matches, board games, elections. This competition requires one to be secret about one's strategies in order to stay 'ahead of the game'. Whatever hurts the other will help you. More and more we have come to realize that, in our complex and interdependent worlds, the game is a non-zero game: the world economy, the Internet, the natural environment. In these spheres we all do well or poorly. We can no longer extract resources from one country in a way that will deplete or even destroy it. What happens in Rwanda affects us all. Nonzero-sum games have completely different strategic implications than zero-sum games, the most important one is transparency — if you know what I am trying to accomplish, we can search together for common gains.

Others who appear similar

If we have difficulty in remaining aware of the profound differences when dealing with cultures so visibly different than our own, how difficult is it then to see the differences between us and people that otherwise look, talk and act like we do? Personality types, learning styles are but two of many dimensions along which people differ, which can cause great grief to the uninitiated. Observe how people behave in a brainstorming session. It is a good viewing ground for profound type differences. Watch the ones that love the exercise, splashing around like little children in a wading pool, one idea follows another, getting more and more outrageous, and the initiators of the ideas seem to get carried away. Now watch the others who are not participating, who try to bring the others down to earth with words like 'no that won't work, have you thought about this, no we already tried that'; and watch the effect these statements have on the others. The scene is set for a collective dragging down, crabs in a pot, whenever one tries to climb out, the rest drag it down, and all stay on the bottom, and will be cooked. As Tom Peters says: 'You don't want the wet noodles dragging down the live wires' (Peters, 1994b: 204). But a little bit later in the process you need those so-called wet noodles to bring back to earth the live wires and make some sense out of the creative chaos. No one type is always the best or always the worst.

The Myers-Briggs Personality Indicator (MBTI) was originally developed to sort people into different types. Four dimensions, with two dichotomous poles, represent a total combination of 16 types. Each type is a dynamic interaction of the ways in which we take in information (through our senses or through intuition) and evaluate information (through logical reasoning or through subjective reasoning) and our orientation towards the external world of people and objects (extroversion) and our own internal world of ideas and associations (introversion). The MBTI is but one, although one of the most exhaustively researched around the world, of many different personality assessment instruments. Another frequently used test in management and leadership training is the Learning Style Inventory, which is based on David Kolb's (1984) experiential learning cycle and helps the user discern his or her preferred style of learning along two dimensions: active versus passive, and concrete versus abstract. Situational leadership theory emphasizes both task and relationship behaviour. The particular style a leader takes is influenced by the maturity of the person being led. The LEAD (Leader Effectiveness and Adaptability Description) instrument was designed to measure self-perception of three aspects of leader behaviour: style, style range and style adaptability. The instrument has been expanded to include a LEAD-Other, to take into account the perception of subordinates, superiors and peers (Hersey and Blanchard, 1982).

There is an almost infinite number of tests, inventories, rating scales and other instruments on the market. Some, like the ones mentioned above, have been well researched and have a host of more or less scientific publications to back them up. Others vary in clarity, reliability and validity. One can now hop onto the Internet and take a variety of tests which are instantly scored and the results fed back (http://www.queendom.com/tests.html). What is important about these instruments is not so much that they will tell you who you are and 'explain' or 'excuse' you, but rather that they provide a vocabulary with which we can describe differences, and present them as gifts that we all bring to a group. Some people claim these terms are not entirely neutral, and may be culturally biased — a notion that is becoming prevalent in South Africa. In organizations, certain traits are usually more valued than others. Any organization benefits from having all types on its staff. However, this diversity also causes stresses in the system. The 'deviant' types are thus at a disadvantage and tend to get blamed for these stresses. In such cases, 'typing' may be risky for an individual. While being mindful of these traps, the practical value of such instruments is that when two parties clash over how to do something, it may have more to do with the way in which information is taken in and processed rather than with who is right and who is wrong. And therefore our task is not so much to quibble over whose leadership to follow, but rather to acknowledge that some kinds of tasks come more naturally to some of us than others — and this may be a way to divide the work or call on someone's strengths.

Metaskill 3: Knowing where you want to go

As an old Chinese proverb says: 'If you don't know where you are going, any way will get you there.' When a group of people argues over what it needs to do, it is nearly always because the members of the group have neglected to agree on a destination point, the result they want, or the vision they are pursuing. Thus, the 'how do we get there' question is unanswerable as long as the 'there' is not defined. This practice is rampant in the world of training: expensive training programmes are put together without a thought about the intended result of the training. Instead, people quibble about which lecturers should come in, what exercises should be done and what books should be read. We see the same phenomenon in employment dissatisfaction: ask people who are drifting in and out of jobs, or feel stuck in their jobs, to describe their ideal job. Chances are that they cannot. Aside from the amount of money they would be making in these imaginary jobs, little is clear, and thus has no power in guiding them. And so they keep drifting, until that time when they know what they want, and then 'all sorts of things occur to help one that would never otherwise have occurred. A whole stream of events issue from the decision, raising in one's favour all manner of unforeseen incidents and meetings, and material assistance, which no man could have dreamed would come his way' (W.H. Murray, leader of the Scottish Himalaya Expedition on the top of Mount Everest, 1958). This happened to Joseph Jaworski. A series of seemingly a-causal events, where he literally bumped into people and things that took him where he needed to go. Carl Gustav Jung called this 'synchronicity'. In his 1952 book, *Synchronicity: An Acausal Connecting Principle*, Jung describes this phenomenon as 'coincidences' that were connected so meaningfully that their 'chance' concurrence would represent a degree of improbability that would have to be expressed by an astronomical figure (Storr, 1983: 339).

Vision is essentially about hope that a transformation is possible. The Dutch futurist Fred Polak noted that in every instance of a flowering culture there had been a positive image of the future at work: without a vision, the culture died. History is full of examples of once vibrant cultures that withered away and finally disappeared. Mandela writes in his autobiography:

> I never lost hope that this grand transformation would occur. Not only because of the great heroes I have already cited, but because of the courage of the ordinary men and women of my country. I always knew that deep down in every human heart, there was mercy and generosity. No-one is born hating another person because of the colour of his skin, or his background, or his religion. People must learn to hate, and if they can

learn to hate, they can be taught to love, for love comes more naturally to the human heart than its opposite.

(Mandela, 1996: 749)

There are two strands coming together here: the knowing where you want to be at some point in the future, and the help that one can receive from the universe in getting there. Note that it is not the help from the university, but rather from the universe that gets you there.

In knowing where we want to be, many of us have been handicapped by our past. In certain countries it is culturally acceptable for women to expect and/or want what others want for them, and often these others are significant males: fathers, uncles, brothers, and later husbands, and eventually sons. No one has asked them what they want, or they have learned very early in life that 'wanting something' is bad. Many women, and men as well, are acting out other people's dreams for them. Many family dramas can be traced to such projected dreams and hopes. This is the risk: when we do not know what we want, we can easily become slaves of other people's desires for us, or other organizations' desires for us. Yet visions do not come that easily. Aside from the inability to think of what you want for yourself (as opposed to what others want for you), there is also reluctance to articulate a vision. As Jean Baker Miller describes (with particular reference to women), 'If you do not know what you want, you can avoid taking the risk to get it' (Baker Miller, 1986: 109). Letting other people decide what you want absolves you from ever taking responsibility for not getting where you wanted to be. And so we are back at knowing what we do not want, and blaming others when we get what we did not want, thus reinforcing the closed loop. It is the illusion of a safe existence. As little birds in a cage, we stay where we are without venturing out. We get fed and taken care of, but we have traded in our deepest longings (without knowing them) for a dependence on caretakers whose commitment we have no control over, and which may not last as long as we think. And then what?

The same forces are at work at an organizational level. If a company does not have vision, and the marketplace or some other outside force determines where the company is going, there may not be a company left (Tregoe, Zimmerman, Smith and Tobia, 1990: 35). We have encountered a variation of this in the small non-profit organizations in the developing world, which are being pushed this way, or that, depending on the latest wishes of their sponsors or donors. When these donors come from different places, the picture gets messier, with power differentials and conflicting paradigms. It is no wonder that such organizations are called 'overdependent on foreign aid', or 'unempowered', or just plain 'incompetent'. How could any organization perform under such circumstances?

And finally, the 'imposed vision' is also at work when an employee finds him- or herself forced to buy into an organizational vision that is not congruent with his or her own vision. Sculley, formerly of Apple Computer, stated to Apple's new employees that 'the new corporate contract is that we'll offer you an opportunity to express yourself and grow, if you promise to leash yourself to our dream, at least for a while' (quoted in Whyte, 1994: 78). That is great if your dreams are in alignment, but it spells trouble if you do not have one. Sometimes we fool ourselves into thinking that we do have a vision. We call it a negative vision: we know what we do not want. However, framing a goal as the absence of something is not very inspiring or motivating, and it severely limits one's circle of allies. In his autobiography, Mandela describes his long-standing opposition to communism: 'I was far more certain in those days of what I was against than what I was for' (Mandela, 1996: 137). It wasn't a very useful stance because it kept him from discovering common ground with the communists, which were, after all, also after a new society. Knowing what we do not want gives little direction for action. The slogan, 'End World Hunger', contains no clues for a visual image. But when we change it to: 'Every child needs three meals a day!' we can begin to form a mental image of a child, happily eating, and a first condition for action is in place — we have a picture of the destination. The Tourism industry knows about this and effectively uses pictures of destinations to propel us into action (saving money, buying tickets, and so on). Effective leaders know about this too — it is not just a marketing trick.

Having a vision of the destination is about passion, about dreaming and about taking responsibility for one's future. This is where the other strand comes in: the open mind to take in the messages from the universe, to allow things to happen. Countless are the stories of people who were searching for meaning, a goal, a vision, when all sorts of things began to present themselves to them, but this did not occur until something happened. Jung blames Cartesian philosophy, which has left us clinging rigidly to its idea of reality, and which has severely limited our view. Native Americans, Native South Africans, Native Australians knew this. Luckily for us, they are spread around the globe and their stories and wisdom are captured in many books and folklore, so we can access it if we want.

Many of the synchronicity stories (those told by Jung, by Jaworski, and events we have experienced for ourselves) revolve around animals. Not long ago, a deer crashed through the glass window of a law office in Boston. In Native American traditions, the deer represents gentleness. It was a clear message from 'out there' to the lawyers, who had probably not been very gentle lately. In the same week, in a well-off town close to Boston, a moose was caught. The moose is the largest and strongest member of the deer family, and is usually not seen in populated areas. If you are attentive to these events, you can receive their messages. Jamie Sams and David Carson have captured the age-old wisdom of animals, derived from the teachings of many Native American tribes in their medicine cards (Sams and Carson, 1988). According to them, the moose may have been there to remind us that 'in tooting your own horn you have failed to be interested in others, and have therefore forgotten that everyone teaches everyone else in some way . . . moose medicine may be asking you to grow quiet for a while, to calm your spirit and allow the strength and wisdom of silence to enter your heart' (1988: 82).

Those of us who live along paved roads, in concrete and brick structures far from the wild, have lost this connection with animals and nature, so essential to humankind. According to Eagle Chief (Letakots-Les) who headed the Pawnee tribe in the United States in the late nineteenth century:

> In the beginning of all things, wisdom and knowledge were with the animals, for Tirawa [the Native American Pawnee tribe's 'father' spirit], the One Above, did not speak directly to man. He sent certain animals to tell men that he showed himself through the beasts, and that from them, and from the stars and the sun and the moon man learns . . . all things tell of Tirawa.

So the animals come crashing in on us, in a desperate attempt to get our attention. The strength of a vision derives from the passion and enthusiasm behind it. It is this passion that moves mountains, or, as in Mandela's case, abolishes apartheid, something that seemed too high a mountain to climb for so long. Few of us can imagine staying focused through a quarter of a century of incarceration. And it is in the word 'enthusiasm' that we find the Greek roots of *en-theos*, the God within, the divine hand that guides us to where we want to be, the absolute faith that what we want is possible. We have observed a relationship between having a vision and a sense of self-worth and self-esteem, both at a personal and at an organizational level. When there is no sense of purpose, and when the self-esteem is missing, the love of power and privilege rushes eagerly to fill the void, and we end up with the director driving around in a big fancy car, using money for the wrong things and robbing the organization of whatever idealism and goodwill it had. Such an organization needs a good dose of passion and purpose in the form of a shared vision. Then it can play and dance again!

Creating a shared vision

The process of visioning is fairly new, and, by some, considered a fad. And yet, seeing a group piece together a common vision is a powerful experience. Sometimes there are surprises, when statements appear that relate to how the people in the organization are working together. Traditionally, when companies or organizations established goals, these were usually external and often quantitative: market share, profit, stock value, size of audience, targets reached. But with the process of collective visioning a new element has been added: the element of the individual's dream for a better future. The power of such a visioning process is that it *hooks into fundamental individual aspirations*. When this collective exercise is preceded by an individual visioning exercise, this powerful connection becomes even more marked. Countless are the times that we have seen people moved to the point of tears, and getting back in touch with some very deeply held values, beliefs, and wishes about life, which had been covered over, or buried in the daily routines, or hassles of work — especially in large bureaucracies. In South Africa's Eastern Cape Province, a group of health professionals from various primary health care (PHC) sub-disciplines, many of whom had never planned anything together, joined forces for two days to come up with a common vision for PHC in their province.

The group was asked to dream a bit and imagine that a reporter, many years from now, would visit their province to report on the extraordinary accomplishments in PHC. What would the story be like? Individuals began to write their own versions first, then compared notes, looked at common themes, and combined the individual stories into one. A powerful story emerged. This story was read aloud in many places after that, and each time it left the group silent, in awe, with big smiles on people's faces, nodding, 'Yes, that's what we want!'

From common ground to common purpose

In South Africa, but not only here, the need to bring together people with different perspectives is critical for future survival. Technology and world economics have connected us in ways that have made the word 'independence' obsolete. 'Interdependence' is the operative word. Our biggest job is to find common ground and then look for the ideas to break through whatever barrier we have imposed on ourselves. This is an inclusive and creative process. Smith (in Senge et al., 1995) describes a process for creating a shared vision that is developmental: 'Every stage of the process should help build both the listening capacity of the leader and the leadership capacities of the rest of the organization' (1995: 313). The stages remind one of the situational leadership model of Hersey and Blanchard (1982), moving from telling, to selling, to testing, consulting to the desired end state of co-creating. Marvin Weisbord uses a large group process called 'future search conference' (Weisbord and Janoff, 1995) as a method of getting to this shared vision in the latest stage of co-creating. In her book *Winning through participation* Laura Spencer describes another process that allows a large group to create a vision together, using an inductive process that departs from the individual dreams (Spencer, 1989).

Love and work

What is important here is that vision, whether individual or organizational, animates, inspires, transforms us only if it is deeply rooted in our human needs and values. And the essential need and value is love (Robert Frost rolled these two together by saying 'love and need are one'). According to Joe Jaworski (1996), love manifests itself in organizations in three ways: love for ourselves, love for others, and love for what we do. James Autry in his book on *Love and Profit*, suggests that good management is largely a matter of love, because proper management involves caring for people, not manipulating them. Wheatley and Kellner-Rogers (1996) say that love is a potent source of power, because we inhabit a quantum universe that knows nothing of itself, independent of its relationships. Fromm (1956) says that love is not primarily a relationship to a specific person, but an attitude, an orientation of character that determines the relatedness of a person to the world as a whole. This capacity for love is what creates a 'field' around a person, a field that propels oneself towards greater action, a mission, a cause greater than oneself, that transcends individual and selfish needs. Margaret

Wheatley (1996) describes organizational vision in such a way, as a field, 'a force of unseen connections that influences employees' behaviour — rather than as evocative messages about some desired future state'. Mandela felt this as he graduated from Fort Hare University and was drawn into and towards the struggle against racial prejudice (Mandela, 1996: 102). A powerful vision then acts like a lightning rod, giving courage, hope and attracting others who are after the same thing. Such a field is a self-reinforcing phenomenon: the stronger the field, the more people are attracted, the more other people get attracted. Vision is a powerful magnet. But vision is also about creativity. What is possible is infinite. The leader who can bring out ideas in others has an immense advantage. Gary Hamel dismisses the traditional planning in which a small elite group goes off site and plots the company's future. Such a process disempowers the rest of the organization. Whatever the results, few will feel bound by it unless under duress. The new role, according to Hamel and many others, is the one of student, rather than magistrate (Hamel, 1996: 81).

Metaskill 4: Understanding power and group dynamics

Self-awareness is an important prerequisite for appreciating what happens in groups and between groups. As much as we like to pretend that we are all rational beings, making rational decisions about our choices and acting rationally in groups, much of what we actually do is not very rational. Inside groups other people's behaviour triggers off powerful reflexes in us. It activates parent tapes and influences what we say or do, don't say or don't do, in ways of which we are often not very conscious. Group relations training, sometimes referred to as 'sensitivity training', aims to bring these processes into our consciousness by creating temporary systems (workshops) in which the primary task is to learn about ourselves in the here and now, using what happens in the group as our curriculum, syllabus and texts, all rolled into one. These experiences can provoke a lot of anxiety because we have suddenly become the object of study, and so has everyone else in the group, including the group itself, as if it had a mind of its own.

When we work in groups there is usually a task. We clarify the task, come to agreement on what we need to do, and what roles each group member is to play. Initially, we also need to clarify the boundaries: that is how we define who is part of our group and who is not, how to become a member or be kicked out, the time horizon of our group, the place(s) where we meet, and finally how we handle leadership. All of these issues need to be worked out and agreed upon. If anyone of these is not clear, the group will find itself floundering. This is what Bion (1961) calls the work group: a level of functioning at which members consciously pursue an agreed-upon objective and deliberately work towards the completion of a task. But there are also irrational processes at work. Bion used the term 'basic assumption group', which combines the hidden agendas of the group members, their unconscious wishes, fears, defences, fantasies, impulses, and projections. Bion identified three distinct basic assumptions: *dependency* (the group secures security and protection from one individual, usually the leader, and acts as incompetent children who need to be guided by this leader for the survival of the group); *fight/ flight* (fighting among each other, often for leadership, or complete withdrawal from the group in order to survive); and *pairing* (two members of the group pair up to take care of the work and secure the survival of the group). The work group focuses outward, the assumption group inward. The tension between the two is always there, sometimes referred to as 'task and process'. It helps to recognize these phenomena in groups. They may explain why a group is lost or not making any progress. Understanding group dynamics provides a language to make the group process discussable, so that the unconscious choices can be made more conscious, 'do we really want to be so completely dependent on the leader?'

Intergroup behaviour is subjected to the same dynamics, and recognizing irrational processes can help to overcome conflict, irritation and allow true dialogue to develop. Common intergroup irrational processes are *social projection* (your group has all the undesirable characteristics that this group cannot accept of itself), *scapegoating* (heaping all the blame and 'sins of the forefathers' on one group or person) and *stereotyping* (the group you belong to has certain characteristics, because you are a member of that group, you have them too!).

Many models exist of group development over time. Most of us remember the apprehension, anxiety and politeness that is so palpable when groups first come together. There is a hesitance to take leadership, to impose opinions and to direct the group. This we have witnessed countless times with the MBA groups at the Graduate School of Business at the University of Cape Town. Then, over time, people take on roles and the politeness begins to make way for little conflicts about how things should be done. As time goes by these conflicts are resolved (or the group dissolves) and a pattern of norms begins to emerge. Finally the group reaches a time of trust, openness and even intimacy facilitating the task of the group. Often there is an end to the group and it dissolves, the members mourn, and join new groups, to start the whole process all over. Anthony Banet (1976) distinguishes three different models of group development theory: the linear model, the helical model and the cyclical model.

Linear model

In the linear model, like the one outlined above, the group is focused on the future and moves through a series of successive stages, each one better than the previous one: forming, storming, norming, performing (and mourning).

The helical model

The helical model describes group development as a progressive deepening of the relationships, with a focus on the past, the process followed is that of a helix, a spiraling in, deeper and deeper. Most psychotherapy groups follow this model.

The cyclical model

In the cyclical model, the focus is on the here and now, the present, and the individuals become aware of the polarities that operate in the group. According to Banet 'the model links human events with other natural phenomena and teaches the ancient philosophy of Tao, which aims for personal centredness and integrity in a world of turmoil and conflict' (Banet, 1976: 178).

What scares people most about groups is the potential for conflict and the degree to which they bring out irrational and unwanted behaviour in oneself and create discomfort, or worse, embarrassment. Learning to read a group, and see both its rational and irrational processes at work, makes working in groups less mysterious and more manageable. When one is under attack as the leader of a group, it helps to know that the fight assumption is activated, or that we are in the storming mode. It helps if one can name that, without threatening or embarrassing the group — sometimes simply by stopping and reflecting on one's own feelings ('I feel really under siege') or the process ('We seem to be stuck, and as people tune out, fewer and fewer are left to help us get unstuck'). This 'stop-action' allows us to make an appeal to people's sense of responsibility, resurrect the vision if there was one, or create one if there was none, and get things back on track. Not being aware of group dynamics and group development leads to self-doubt ('I can never do this'; 'I am incompetent'), a feeling of victimization ('Poor me') and paranoia ('They're after me'), frustration and anger, and all the ineffective and futile actions that are inspired by these feelings.

So, to conclude, the metacognitions are second-order cognitions: thoughts about thoughts, knowledge about knowledge and reflections about actions (Silver, 1993). Metaskills are the skills that help us get to these metacognitions. Although we looked at various areas in which leaders need to develop awareness, the topic does not lend itself easily to a linear presentation. The same themes emerge over and over again, and each area is connected to any other. Awareness in one area increases awareness in another, it is an exponential process and experience — the awareness gets bigger in leaps and bounds. This chapter is not about prescriptions, yet it is full of them. It tells you to act, while it emphasizes being. It claims to talk about skills that aren't really skills. It suggests reflection but urges action. It tells you what you should do while emphasizing that no one can create a vision for anyone else. We have tried to change you, even just fractionally, while implying that you are the only one who can change yourself. This chapter is full of paradoxes that do not need to be resolved, but awareness of these paradoxes, we believe, is *critically* important.

It is so easy to become someone you do not want to be, even without realizing that it is happening. 'We are created by the choices we make every day. And if we take action in order to please some authority-figure, we'll suddenly wake up down the road and say: "This isn't me. I never wanted to be this person"' (Siegel, 1996: 42). The challenge is to live authentically — be real.

Kate Wolff was a Canadian singer and songwriter who died of cancer in her early forties. From a tremendous legacy of songs we have singled out one line that could serve as a motto for this chapter: 'Find out what you really care about, then live a life that shows it.' This is the task. It requires us to do more of all those things we have dropped along the way as we are rushing to our destination: live by example, tell the truth, keep our promises, be fair, respect each other, encourage curiosity, sit down, listen, watch, learn, be open to the messages from the universe, let go of tightly defined outcomes, embrace error, relax, hand over the stick, believe in others, ask, and finally, never make it rough on people, life is rough enough. Our academic or business education may not have prepared us for these simple precepts. We know how to lecture, initiate, interrupt others, talk down, and discuss. All of these words come from a paradigm that is beginning to lose its usefulness.

Openness
The Times are a-Changing

> The new leadership will not be provided by 'take charge' elite, but will emerge from the capacity that lies within each and every person. It will be a leadership that does not presume to have all the answers, but one that seeks to empower others to work on their own problems. It will be a leadership that skilfully provokes and accompanies people and organizations as they undertake their difficult work.
>
> *Beerel, 1998*

These are unparalleled times in the history of global business. Technology and an increased acceptance of economic freedom are ensuring that every conceivable barrier is being broken down. Businesses today are very different from what they were ten years ago, and will probably be even less recognizable by the end of the next decade. In South Africa this change is being magnified by the incredible political, social and economic transition, which started in the 1990s and is continuing at the start of this new century.

In times of great transition, leadership becomes critically important, and the magnitude of today's changes will demand not only more leadership, but new approaches to leadership. It is critical then that leaders are open to new ways of doing things. Prominent American pundit John Kotter (1990) argues that in the turbulent fast-changing environment of the 1990s, it is leadership, not just plain old management, that is required. Charles Handy (1998), the leading UK commentator on management, attributes the growing interest in leadership in recent years to an underlying change in the way we actually think about organizations. He suggests that, in the past, we thought of organizations as 'flawed' pieces of engineering, but capable in theory of perfectibility. Today, however, we use a different kind of language when talking about organizations — a language which uses such terms as 'networks', 'alliances', 'culture' and 'shared values'. This, Handy argues, is the language of leadership, not of management. It is also a reflection of the shift from a Newtonian way of seeing the world, which, for much of the past century, has used machine-like imagery in our perspectives on human behaviour.

Quantum theory, according to which all is not what it seems, is the new lens through which commentators such as Margaret Wheatley (1992; 1999), Ralph Stacey (1991; 1992; 1995; 1996) and Joseph Jaworski (1996), are now observing the process of leadership. Changing times are forcing us to rethink our ideas on leadership. Hill (1998: 3) provides us with a useful framework on changed theoretical assumptions within the field of leadership. Her framework draws on the work of a number of contemporary writers, including Conger (1993); Coulsen-Thomas (1997), Covey (1995; 1997); Gilliland, Tynan and Smith (1996); McCollum (1995); Merry (1995); Nel (1994); Senge (1995a; 1995b; 1996); Saunders (1998); Stacey (1996); Townsend and Gebhardt (1997); and Van der Merwe (1994).

Although the shifts outlined in Table 2.1 should be taken as theoretical tendencies rather than as indicative of widespread business realities or even representative of the bulk of theoretical literature, they nevertheless suggest dramatic changes in outlook.

Encapsulated in the Newtonian vs. quantum perspectives, is the age-old debate on the differences between management and leadership. The view has long been held that management is about providing the order and procedures necessary to cope with the complexity of organizations. Managers see themselves as conservators and regulators of an existing order of affairs with which they personally identify, and from which they gain rewards. A manager's sense of self-worth is often enhanced by perpetuating and strengthening existing institutions. Traditionally, leadership, by contrast, is about coping with change and has been seen as a more strategic concept. The simple analogy adapted from Stephen Covey (1989) is that the manager ensures that the organization is able to move up a step ladder, the leader ensures that the ladder is resting against the correct wall! Hence, if there is a change to be made, it will be the leader who drives this process. But are the concepts of leadership and management really that distinct?

Professor Albert Zaleznik (1992), a psychoanalyst and the Konosuke Matsushita Professor of Leadership Emeritus at Harvard Business School, dismisses the idea that, through training, it is possible to develop people to be both effective managers and effective leaders. He argues that they are very different kinds of people, with different motivation, different personal histories and different ways of thinking and acting. He claims that 'a managerial culture emphasizes rationality and control. Whether his or her energies are directed towards goals, resources, organization structures, or people, a manager is a problem solver' (Zaleznik, 1992: 127). Zaleznik goes further, by claiming that managers tend to adopt impersonal, if not passive, attitudes toward goals, and that managerial goals arise out of necessities rather than desires, and therefore 'are deeply embedded in their organization's history and culture'.

Peters and Waterman (1982) talk of the manager as cop, referee, devil's advocate, dispassionate analyst, professional, decision maker, naysayer and pronouncer. For Peters, leadership, by contrast, is about being a cheerleader, enthusiast, nurturer of champions, hero finder, wanderer, dramatist, coach, facilitator and builder. His role models for leadership are people like Bill Hewlett of Hewlett Packard, Steve Jobs of Apple Computer and Sam Walton of Walmart. Given these observations, in the South African context we might argue that during the presidency of Nelson Mandela, he led South Africa, while Thabo Mbeki, as

Table 2.1
*Transition in leadership theory**

1940s Traits	1950s Task and relationships	1960s Contingencies	1970s Leader– follower inter- action	1980s Transform- ation and vision	1990s Credibility and soul

World-view

A controllable, predictable world Newtonian science	A systemic, complex world with multiple causality

Organizational philosophy

Organization as a machine	Organization as a self-organizing community

Time orientation

Future orientation	Respect for the future, regard for the present and understanding of the past

Role of the leader

Plan, control and organize	Steward, teacher, designer, facilitator and catalyst

Leadership power base

Positional power	Referent power (and positional power)

Activities of the leader

Analyse a problem, solve it, sell the solution to others and manage the implementation of the solution	Formulate a vision and create an environment that enables the achievement of the vision

Follower role

Followers as a means of production	Followers as the key source of information and creativity
Instrumentalism	Humanism

Source of wisdom

Leader	Followers and the organizational system

Outcome of leader–follower interaction

Compliant followers dependent on the leader	Committed, empowered followers
Attainment of profit	Profit as well as stewardship of employees, the organization and society.

*Adapted from Hill, 1998.

Deputy President, managed the country. But is this to say that Mbeki is not a leader? Is there not scope then for leadership to take its form in different ways?

If we accept the link between leadership and change, it can be argued that in the South African corporate environment there is a glaring lack of leadership. The imperatives for change are clear; international competition and the need for employment equity are the flagbearers showing us what is needed. Yet there is a sense that these concepts are incompatible in the South African context. We may attribute this to the inherent conservatism that characterizes organizations, and the natural resistance that people have to change. As John D. Rockefeller (1973: 72) puts it: 'An organization is a system with a logic of its own, and all the weight of tradition and inertia. The deck is stacked in favour of the tried and proven way of doing things and against the taking of risks and striking out in new directions.' We might take this American perspective on organizations to explain away the inertia that is evident in South African organizations. This inertia is reflected by figures from the Breakwater Monitor, a research project at the University of Cape Town's Graduate School of Business, which tracks employment equity in a sample of companies that in total employ more than a million people. The latest figures from this research indicate that 13,78 % of management in South Africa are women, and 12,5 % of management are black (that is, African, Asian, and Coloured). However, of these figures, only 6,45 % in senior management are either black or women (little wonder the emphasis that a black government is placing on employment equity). The situation is not surprising, given the comments of management consultant, Martin Nasser, who in the early 1990s wrote that real participative management among South African executives is a rarity, particularly in the classical sense of the word. Nasser and Vivier (1993) identified what they saw as a hybrid style of leadership among the majority of South African organizations they studied. They described this as a mixture between a 'benevolent dictatorship' and a 'cultivated autocracy'. Either way, the sense of a top–down leadership paradigm is clear. This perspective has been reinforced by our own research five years later, in which we interviewed thirty-five leaders from large organizations in different sectors. The autocratic, paternalistic approach is still present, although undoubtedly the history of the country is a critical influence.

As Anthony Coombe, Cape Town senior partner of Price Waterhouse Coopers puts it: 'The pressures on leaders and senior managers in South Africa are immense, because there is a thinner line of really senior leaders in this country than there should be. And that's for historical reasons, and also because we're losing so many good people to emigration' (April, 1997). Does enormous pressure under which leaders find themselves force the adoption of an autocratic approach? Is the heroic figure of the leader the most appropriate image of the organizational leader today? Is there really any alternative? We may argue that it really is up to the influence a leader exerts in altering moods, evoking images and expectations, and in establishing specific desires and objectives, that determines the direction an organization takes. That they are active instead of reactive, shaping ideas instead of responding to them, and that they adopt a personal and active attitude towards goals. A recent example of this is the demutualization of Old Mutual, South Africa's largest insurance company, essentially a process driven by the senior leadership in the organization, led by Chairman Mike Levett. The net result of this influence changes the way people think about what is desirable, possible, and necessary. But does such an influence generate optimal energy for the organization? At the end of the day, the question remains: is the authoritarian approach the most effective? Newton would probably have said 'yes', given the perspective that people are all really just like machines. Is the fact that people are not like machines adequate grounds for a more participative approach to leadership?

The irony is that the transition from authoritarianism to participation requires firm guidance by leaders who have been appointed or elected to exercise authority. This may seem like a contradiction, but the long and difficult transition process stands little chance of succeeding unless it is driven by those who wield power. Only with their committed support can the old structure, built on leadership and management supremacy, worker dependence and subordination, be dismantled.

Colin Hall, executive chairman of Wooltru, a large group of retail companies in South Africa, makes the point that 'leadership is a constant requirement of a healthy environment — leadership, in the sense that it will be shared across all sorts of people, at all sorts of levels in organizations and elsewhere. What we need to encourage is the capacity that people have to follow with enthusiasm, and to lead people who are following them with enthusiasm' (April, 1997). Hall's view indicates that leadership can be anywhere in the organization. Similarly, Cashman makes the point that:

> We lead by virtue of who we are. Some people . . . will make breakthroughs and then lead their own lives more effectively. Others will develop themselves and passionately lead major organizations to new heights. Whether we are at an early stage in our career, a knowledge-worker or a corporate executive, we are all CEOs of our own lives. The only difference is the domain of influence. The process is the same; we lead from who we are.

Cashman, 1998: 18

Manz and Sims (1993: 140) share this opinion. Their focus is on a new form of leadership — one designed to facilitate the self-leadership energy within each person. Their position is that true leadership comes from within a person, not from the outside. 'Leadership is not something we do. It comes from somewhere inside us. Leadership is a process, an ultimate expression of who we are. It is our being in action. Our being, our personhood, says as much about us as a leader as the act of leading itself' (Cashman, 1998: 18). According to Cashman (1998: 20), '*leadership is authentic self-expression that creates value*'. The implications of this definition are quite far reaching. From this perspective, leadership is not seen as hierarchical — it exists everywhere in organizations. The roles of leadership change, but the core process is the same. Cashman (1998: 20) makes the further point that 'anyone who is authentically self-expressing and creating value, is leading. Some may self-express and create value through ideas, others through systems, others through people, but the essence is the same'. At its best, external leadership provides a spark and supports the flame of the true inner leadership that dwells within each person. At its worst, it disrupts this internal process, causing damage to the person and the constituencies served by the leader. This perspective represents a departure from the dominant and, we think, incomplete view of leadership. It suggests a new measure of a leader's strength — *the ability to maximize the contributions of others through recognition of their right to guide their own destiny*, rather than the ability to bend the will of others to one's own. Leading others to lead themselves means bringing out the best, but mainly in others, not just in oneself. This form of leadership brings out the best that lies within those that surround the formal leader. This view is endorsed by the quantum theorists who see matter as made up of particles and relationships or interconnectedness, both seen and unseen. But if leadership can prevail anywhere in the organization, what of management?

As Professor John Simpson, Head of Management Studies at the University of Cape Town puts it, 'I would make a distinction between management and leadership. One shouldn't, but I'm afraid that one has to . . . because many, many managers in this country aren't leaders. Ideally, of course they should be . . . but very often it's situational, it's historic, it's got to do with previous cultures, it's got to do with recognition of qualifications. All those sorts of things have actually resulted in managers not necessarily being leaders' (April, 1997). Whilst Simpson reluctantly draws the distinction between management and leadership, Zaleznik (1992) is very definite about highlighting the distinction. He suggests that managers prefer to work with others and that they avoid solitary activity because it makes them anxious. 'The need to seek out others with whom to work and collaborate seems to stand out as an important characteristic of managers. However, managers may lack empathy, or the capacity to sense intuitively the thoughts and feelings of others.' Empathy is not simply a matter of paying attention to other people, it is also the capacity to take in emotional signals and make them meaningful in a relationship.

According to Zaleznik, managers relate to people according to the role they play in a sequence of events or in a decision-making process, while leaders, who are concerned with ideas, relate in more intuitive and empathetic ways. Certainly if the intuitive and empathic capacity of Zaleznik's leaders is lacking in managers in South Africa, then the country has a real problem. Given the history of the country, there is no way that the type of change needed will take place without qualities such as intuition and empathy. Perhaps the type of dilemma facing many leaders in South Africa is that voiced by André Harrison, General Manager of Cape Metro Rail, who observed that, 'The organization will only survive because of relationships . . . [however] on a personal level, I don't find relationships that important. I feel that it is part of my work, part of my job . . . but, for me personally, it's not that important' (April, 1997). Research has shown that Harrison is not alone in his perspective. Working in one-to-one relationships, where there is a formal and recognized difference in power of the players, takes a great deal of tolerance for emotional interchange. This interchange, inevitable in close working relationships, probably accounts for the reluctance of many executives to become involved in such relationships. We might argue then, that in the pursuit of leadership, South African leaders may resort to management. It is easier, safer and more clear-cut.

Zaleznik's distinction between management and leadership may be simplistic and misleading. First-class managers are often likely to possess a good measure of leadership as well. Gardner (1993: 160) makes the point that these managers distinguish themselves from run-of-the-mill managers in that the former think in the longer term; they grasp how their unit fits within a larger system; they are able to influence others beyond their jurisdictions and thus can integrate fragmented constituencies; they emphasize intangibles such as vision, values, and intuition; they have good political skills in coping with conflict; and they think in terms of renewal, seeking to revise and improve the status quo. Such qualities, however, do not lead to a single profile or image of an idealized leader. Gardner further maintains that there are many kinds of leaders with unique constellations of personal strengths and attributes, and their effectiveness often represents the matching of strengths with historical contexts and the particular contemporary settings in which they act. Zaleznik, however, goes so far as to say that the distinction is simply between a manager needing to focus on *how* things get done, and a leader on *what* gets done, *what* the events and decisions mean to participants. John Simpson's hesitant support for the distinction may be interpreted to mean that South African organizations are underled and overmanaged. Business consultant Laurence Kuper, writing in the South African national newspaper *The Sunday Independent* (1998), made a similar assertion: 'In South Africa, we have too many managers and not enough leaders.' Given the complexity of the history and change that is taking place in South Africa, and the increasingly complex global marketplace, the notion of being underled is daunting. Dealing with complexity requires intuition, empathy, creativity, flexibility and support — qualities more in line with the principles of quantum theory and evolutionary biology than Newtonian physics. The challenge to rethink our approaches to leadership in South Africa is inescapable. Yet perhaps the challenge is simpler than we think. There is undoubted complexity inherent in a country with 11 official languages, a multitude of cultures and a history of autocratic oppression. Appreciating that there can be simplicity in how we approach leadership is possibly the first step. The next step is to determine how we can achieve that simplicity out of complexity. The new sciences, as discussed in the next chapter, provide some insights into how that may be achieved.

Simplicity
New Science and Leadership

We will not understand life and living organisms until we understand emergence. None of us has a solid grasp of emergence, far less a full definition. Emergence is multifaceted, and if you try to be too precise, you will lose what you're after. You can't draw an easy border around it. It's like love. No philosopher or novelist would try to define love, would they? Emergence can be described as a holistic phenomenon because the whole is more than the sum of the parts.

John Holland in Lewin and Regine, 1999

In searching for new ways of leading, science, long esteemed by business as a source of technological innovation, may ultimately prove of greatest value to leaders as a source for useful new ways of looking at the world. The situation today is similar to that which existed in the seventeenth century. At that time, the premises of science presented by Isaac Newton, Francis Bacon and René Descartes replaced the Ptolemaic paradigm that had reigned in science until then. Today we are beginning to realize that currently held notions and principles of science do reflect reality, but only part of reality — the ordered, linear, predictable, controllable side of reality.

The new sciences, chaos and complexity theories, have enlightened us to the fact that there are also other aspects of the world in which non-linearity, interactiveness, chaos, complexity, unpredictability and uncertainty are natural, inevitable elements of this universe. Quantum theory is the new lens through which commentators such as Margaret Wheatley, Annabel Beerel, Ralph Stacey and Richard Pascal are now observing the process of leadership. The new rules of complex behaviour, as described by cutting-edge scientific research, have intriguing parallels with the organizational behaviours that many organizations are trying to encourage. Leadership is now being examined for its relational aspects — more and more studies focus on followership, empowerment, leader accessibility, ethics and morals, information sharing, values, vision, and culture. In motivational theory, our attention is shifting from the enticement of external rewards to the intrinsic motivators that spring from the work itself — refocusing on deep longings we have for community, meaning, dignity, and love in our organizational lives.

The shift in thinking

Through the ages, the basic tenets of science have been the underlying assumptions on which we have built our understanding, and much of our view of the world is predicated on a seventeenth-century metaphor — the clockwork universe. Within many organizational structures and academic disciplines we have used the notion that things can be taken apart and then put back together again without any significant loss. 'Old' science, until recently and led by physics, artificially isolated systems in order to study them and dealt with ideal models that are difficult to find in nature. In that mindset, we have broken organizations into functions, and we have broken people into roles. The assumption is that by comprehending the workings of each piece, the whole can be understood — an assumption characterized by materialism and reductionism, and a focus on things rather than relationships. As Margaret Wheatley puts it, in our work lives, we are trying to predict the unpredictable, to manage the unmanageable, and control the uncontrollable (Wheatley, 1992). This bedrock is, however, currently being questioned. New science, the science of chaos theory, evolution biology, quantum mechanics and field theory, deals with systems that display non-linearity and are interdependent with other systems. Most systems in the world are like this. What the new sciences do for us is to see systems and organizations as wholes, not just as collections of parts. Taking a holistic look at things is what dismantles the age-old functional hierarchies and replaces them with cross-functional teams and communities, conducive to lifelong learning. Leaders need to get to know the dynamic behavioural states their organizations are in, and be able to adjust their leadership- and managerial styles to the conditions of their particular state.

Nature has so many things that we crave in organizations, for example, enormous diversity, complexity, flexibility and adaptability. Life self-organizes, and its natural tendency is to organize into greater levels of complexity to support more diversity and greater sustainability (Wheatley and Kellner-Rogers, 1996). Networks, patterns, and structures emerge without external imposition or direction — organization wants to happen. People are intelligent, adaptive, self-organizing, and meaning-seeking. Social systems are purposeful systems with purposeful parts — the parts, as well as the whole, have the choice of ends as well as means (Ackoff, 1994). Therefore, interaction between purposeful parts can take many forms, including conflict and cooperation (Stacey, 1992). Today scientists are developing powerful descriptions of the ways complex systems cope effectively with uncertainty and rapid change, from swarms of mosquitoes to computer programs to future traders in commodity markets. These descriptions provide opportunities for fruitful dialogue between the world of leadership and the world of science. We therefore need to take a fresh look at our theory and practice.

What are these new theories?

The word 'chaos' has for centuries and, for most people and organizations, been viewed as something to avoid. Dominant Western thought has been built around the notion of avoiding chaos. For others, chaos has been a cry of rebellion against this philosophy, for example 'technology communities', on the World Wide Web (www) and Internet, formed to discuss issues around chaos. Most websites on the World Wide Web that use the word 'chaos' in their title, promote ideas of anarchy, randomness, and personal freedom. Chaos theory represents neither of these attitudes, which can be considered linked to the traditional or linear models. It does, however, have something to say about both. Chaos theory is actually a part of the 'new sciences'. That new science is more fully described by titles given to it by scientists, such as Nobel laureate and co-founder of the Santa Fé Institute, Murray Gell-Mann — he calls it the study of complex adaptive systems in his book, *The Quark and the Jaguar.*

When they hear 'new science', many people think about the science of chaos. But chaos is only the tip of the iceberg. According to Ralph Stacey (1995: 481), 'chaos deals with bounded uncertainty and unpredictable change, but is one of a number of new sciences of no less importance'. Some of these are:

- complexity that deals with the common features of complex systems of different sorts;
- the science of self-organization, that explains how novel structures and forms emerge;
- fractals — a geometry, or pattern, of natural and living forms; and
- complex adaptive systems, which is the science of complex systems that are capable of changing themselves to adapt to a changing environment.

Other scientists, such as Ilya Prigogine, Stuart Kauffman, Christopher Langton, John Holland at the Sante Fé Institute in New Mexico, researchers at the Center for Complex Studies at the University of Illinois, and Brian Goodwin at the Open University in the United Kingdom, call the discipline 'complex systems theory', 'complexity theory', 'dynamical systems theory', and 'the study of complex non-linear systems'.

Formally, chaos theory is defined as the study of complex non-linear dynamic systems. 'Complex' implies just that, 'non-linear' implies recursion and higher mathematical algorithms, and 'dynamic' implies non-constant and non-periodic. The new sciences come from the disciplines of mathematics, physics, biology and chemistry, and from theories of evolution and chaos that span several disciplines. In new science, as is the case in systems thinking and complexity theory, the underlying currents are a movement toward holism, toward understanding the system as a system and focusing on the relationships that exist among the seemingly discrete parts. We are moving to a scientific world-view of systems that look like whirlpools through which matter, energy and information flow (Wheatley, 1992). Chaos theory predicts that complex non-linear systems are inherently unpredictable — but, at the same time, chaos theory also insures that often the way to express such an unpredictable system lies not in exact equations, but in *representations of the overall behaviour of the system* — in plots of strange attractors, fractals and patterns.

The most commonly held misconception about chaos theory is that it is about disorder. One of the central concepts of new science and chaos theory is that, while it is impossible to predict exactly the state or exact future outcome of a system, it is generally quite possible, even easy, to model the overall behaviour of a system. Thus, these theories lay emphasis not on the disorder of the system, the inherent unpredictability of a system, but on *the order inherent in the system*, the universal behaviour of similar systems. In spite of what we may have been taught, the fact is that chaos and order are not opposites from which to choose. They are sides of the same coin of reality, forever interpenetrated and inseparably entwined. The term 'chaos' in new science and complexity theory is order — not simply just order, but the very essence of order.

The new view of reality

The quantum mechanical view of reality strikes against most of our notions of reality, but it is a world in which relationships are the key determinants of what is observed and of how particles manifest themselves. Particles come into being and are observed *only in relationship to something else*. These unseen connections between what were previously thought to be separate entities are the fundamental elements of all creation (Wheatley and Kellner-Rogers, 1996). Our old views constrain and deprive us from engaging fully with this universe of potentialities. We have confused order with control. Our concept of organizations is moving away from mechanistic creations to more fluid, organic structures, even boundaryless organizations.

Let's think, for example, about one important aspect of organizational life — power. Because power is an energy, it contains a charge, positive or negative. What gives power its particular charge, is the nature of the current relationship it is in. Wheatley (1999: 40) informs us that 'when power is shared in such workplace redesigns as participative management and self-managed teams, positive creative power abounds'. Those of us who have been privileged enough to experience such workplace redesigns, will attest to the positive impact of these new relationships, personal satisfaction, increased energy, heightened passion and the resultant symptom — significant increases in productivity.

In other workplaces, leaders attempt to force better results through coercion, competition, and by establishing rank. Wheatley (1999) tells us that in such organizations, a high level of energy is also created, but it is entirely negative. 'Power becomes a problem, not a capacity. People use their creativity to work against these leaders, or in spite of them; they refuse to contribute positively to the organization' (1999: 40).

Instead of imposed control, we see the organization as *existing in the relationships among the people* involved in the organization and, more essentially, in the *quality of those relationships*. The challenge for future leaders who want to be successful, will become one of stewardship and servanthood (Spears, 1995). Gary Oliver, Director of Law for Local Government in the Western Cape Province, South Africa, attributes his organization's current success to the investment that all the staff has made in fostering positive relationships (April, 1997). When this fundamental shift of mind occurs, our sense of identity shifts too, and we begin to accept each other as legitimate human beings.

Systems are self-organizing and they have an organization unto themselves. It is important to allow these organizational systems to emerge and develop. Stacey (1996) asserts that continuous disequilibrium forces systems to change and accommodate a continual influx of information. What this tells us, is that leaders should not impose stability upon their organizations but should discover the relationships in their organization and *look for the organizational system that is already present in the systems they lead*. Thus, effective leaders do not seek stability, instead they search within their organization for the 'hidden', self-organizing principles, rather than impose organization upon the system. They actively seek new information — *continuously scanning the organizational landscape*. In the quantum world, relationships are all there is to reality. Identifying, encouraging, facilitating and nurturing those relationships is the true work of leaders of the twenty-first century.

The way forward with new metaphors

As we leave behind our machine models and look more deeply into the dynamics of living systems, we begin to glimpse an entirely new way of understanding fluctuations, disorder and change. Chaos and order are now understood as mirror images, one containing the other — a continual process within which a system can leap into chaos and unpredictability, yet within that state be held within parameters that are well ordered and predictable. Physics and thermodynamics leads to the understanding of self-organizing systems and system states (equilibrium, near equilibrium, the edge of chaos, and chaos). The second law of thermodynamics states that a closed system in equilibrium is a dying system. Systems which cannot go outside of themselves cannot change, and will certainly wear themselves down until they die. One might argue that this is what happened to apartheid in South Africa. Unless some force is injected into a system, it will spiral down until it dies. We see a clear implication for systems leadership in this law — equilibrium must be avoided in systems, as disequilibrium leads to growth. Garth Eagle, training manager of oil company Caltex (South Africa), says that if you do not have some sort of disequilibrium, even personal and internal disequilibrium, you are never going to change or grow (April, 1997). Change, while often resisted, is necessary to keep the system from the death spiral seen in a closed system.

The concept of entropy is actually the physicists' application of the concept of evolution to physical systems (Prigogine and Stengers, 1984). The greater the entropy of a system, the more highly evolved is the system. Complexity theory is also having a major impact on quantum physics and attempts to reconcile the chaos of quantum physics with the predictability of Newton's universe. The push for such unification came from Einstein. With complexity theory, the distinctions between these sciences are now disappearing. Complexity theory is already affecting critical aspects of our lives. For instance, the understanding of heart arrhythmias and brain functioning has been revolutionized by complexity research. There have been a number of 'toys' developed from complexity research, such as the SimLife and SimAnt series of computer programs. In mathematics, there is lots of work being done on the use of strange attractors, fractals, cellular automa, and other non-linear, graphical mathematical models for studying data that was previously thought of as random. Fractal mathematics is critical to improved information compression and encryption schemes needed for computer networking and telecommunications, so vital for business today. We even see the inception of the quantum computer — a computer capable of parallel processing with processing speeds only dreamt of previously, and having the ability to hold multiple states simultaneously (unlike the current transistorized on-off switches). In biology, recent research involves the use of non-mechanistic models and the identification of new evolutionary processes leading to understanding the genetic algorithm, artificial life simulations, better understanding of learning processes in systems including the brain, and studies of such previously unresearchable areas as consciousness and the mind. Genetic algorithms are being applied to economic research and stock predictions, and engineering applications range from factory scheduling to product design.

Each of these sciences tells us that we cannot continue our mechanistic view of the organization. If we try to control the individual parts of the system, we are bound only for frustration and disappointment. Scientists representing numerous fields of study, for example quantum physics, environmental ecology, and biogenetics have demonstrated conclusively that the universe is more like a great living organism than some huge mechanical contraption — we cannot observe anything without interacting with it. It will only be when we see the system as a whole, that we become effective leaders and managers. In self-organizing systems theory, we must be aware that *only the broadest of rules should be laid down*. Autonomy will then allow the system to become whatever is necessary at the time. New science is also making us more aware that our yearning for simplicity is one that we share with natural systems. In many systems, scientists now understand that order, conformity and shape are not created by complex controls, but by the presence of a *few* guiding principles.

The new sciences are being heralded by a growing constituency of leading-edge thinkers as a major catalyst for the most monumental paradigmatic shift in the history of humankind. Chaos has already permeated the deliberations and practice of virtually every scientific discipline, hard and soft. However, the science of leadership, management and organization is the peculiar exception. Despite the fact that the machine metaphor has been all but abandoned by twentieth-century science, most of us continue to clutch to the reassuring image of the clockwork organization as we move into the twenty-first century. While the old science, rooted as it is in the metaphor of the clockwork, has not been altogether forsaken, the slice of the world to which it remains applicable is but a sliver of the vast whole. We are not cogs in a timepiece, but integral participants in a distinctly living, growing and ever-changing whole being. Isn't it about time we changed our metaphor? While the first item on leaders' agendas for this millennium must be to don the powerful 'spectacles' of chaos, this feat will prove impossible as long as the beliefs and assumptions upon which our careers and organizations have been built remain intact. Colin Hall, executive chairman of South African retail giant Wooltru, claims that 'nobody wants to use a bad lens if they can find a better one' (April, 1997). So far, there has been no sign of a rush to relinquish the images, practices and guiding principles with which society, as a whole, in the Western World has enjoyed such a long and profitable relationship.

New science implications for leaders

Leaders currently treat orderly, predictable linear systems as if they are what is normal and regular. Because it has 'worked' for them in the past, they see no immediate need for changing or embracing new ideas and methods. During our research, in which we interviewed thirty-five leaders in South African organizations, we discovered that most of the leaders had no idea of the theories and the implications of new science, chaos theory and complexity theory. Listed in Exhibit A are some of the responses to the question: 'What do you understand by chaos theory and the new sciences?

However, our research revealed that a few leaders have heard of chaos theory, but only had a vague idea of its implications for organizations and leadership. Some of their responses to the same question ('What do you understand by chaos theory and the new science?') are listed in Exhibit B.

It is interesting to note that only two of the interviewed leaders, actually knew about the organizational and personal implications of such leading-edge theories as chaos theory and new science. We would guess that a similar survey amongst leaders in most industrialized nations of the world would also render limited insights into theories such as chaos theory and the new sciences. This, however, is not to undermine what we see as the important role that such theories can play in developing effective leadership.

New science, chaos and complexity theory challenges all leaders to rethink their most fundamental perspectives and assumptions. It encourages new forms of leadership — forms in which leaders should *allow for multiple goals, embrace the concept of multiple effects and multiple causes within fluid and flexible frameworks;*

forms in which understanding interrelationships, rather than just cause-and-effect, becomes critical. An ancient Sufi teaching captures this shift in focus: 'You think because you understand *one* you must understand *two*, because one and one makes two. But you must also understand *and*.' When systems and business processes are viewed from this perspective, the organization enters an entirely new landscape of connections, of phenomena that cannot be reduced to simple cause and effect. Leaders of organizations often seek stability as a matter of course for their organizations. A stable work force, a stable mission — stability, in general, is for many leaders the utmost goal to be sought. We would argue that to seek stability is to ask for the certain demise of the system.

Exhibit A

Comments of leaders to the question: 'What do you understand by chaos theory and the new science?'

- Frankly, not very much, because I am not very familiar with it. I read the document [you provided], but I think that I should really have got access to other documentation as well. Maybe you should explain to me what I should be seeing in chaos theory.
- Very little actually. I would have thought that it suggests that there isn't a pattern to things and that what happens is entirely random . . . and that must have some throw on strategy.
- I must admit, I have not heard of new science.
- I'm not aware of either of those theories.
- I don't know what one talks about when one talks of new science. I thought that all science was new.
- I frankly don't have any great understanding about it at all, or any great interest in it.
- It must be a new concept since I did my studies.
- Well, I didn't understand anything until I read your brief synopsis. It's a new concept to me.
- Not a great deal — I briefly read an article some time ago that broadly outlined some thinking about chaos theory. It really did not appeal to me, and I also felt it could be used as a 'cop out' in a situation where a decision would have to be made or some definite accountability was required for actions taken.
- I was not aware of chaos theory and complexity theory until I received your brief synopsis.

It is becoming increasingly apparent to many leaders in South Africa that, in order to plan, facilitate and coordinate organizational development and change, in the face of increasing uncertainty across the national cultural boundaries, many

Exhibit B

Comments of some partially informed leaders to the question: 'What do you understand by chaos theory and the new science?'

- Chaos theory is something that I really read about briefly . . . you know, the old cliché about the butterfly in China.
- Well, I know a little bit about chaos theory, in terms of its existence and that things seem to organize themselves reasonably out of what looks like an unreasonable bit of chaos. Somehow things seem to group themselves together . . . it's natural . . . it's something that takes place, but I have not heard about chaos theory related to leadership and organizational behaviour.
- I've always understood that an organization has no shape and form that is permanent, but is an amoeba-type organization where things move, change, break-away, rejoin.
- One doesn't have to have a super hierarchy, and slow, structured change with hierarchical thinking. It's moving towards a tremendously flat organization that is driven by continual change and continual improvement.
- I think it is very practical. It explains a lot of things that the other sciences don't explain. All of a sudden you understand the full spectrum of things, where we are now, and what the shortcomings of the other sciences were.
- One reads on things like the thriving on chaos, and one hears that sort of thing. I don't really know it by name, but guess that it is part of business now. Businesses are not as organized as they used to be, and businesses are getting more chaotic.
- Chaos theory is built into our management principles — letting conflict run its course, letting leadership develop rather than forcing it upon people, and that kind of stuff.

problems must be evaluated and solved. Not only are there language barriers, but entire value systems of employees in South African organizations must be taken into consideration. Many leaders have realized that the autocratic, dictatorial and paternalistic leadership models of the past may not be entirely relevant in a country which has opted to embrace political democracy, union participation, cultural diversity, and involvement of individuals at all levels of the organization. Perhaps the time has come in South Africa where, in order to be successful, it is essential to find areas of common appreciation or interest between those who lead organizations and those who *willingly* follow them. Leaders will, and must, find ways to show respect for the unique differences of individuals to facilitate the process, by being responsive to the values and preferences of people working in various organizations (Jaworski, 1996). Leaders will have to find ways to establish a foundation on the shared values of people, to build a common vocabulary in a nation where eleven languages are officially recognized, and to organize and facilitate employee involvement teams and communities to create innovative ways to change or improve processes of the past. We are only starting to recognize how critical diversity — diverse people, diverse ideas, diverse cultures, diverse interests, diverse backgrounds, diverse qualifications etc. — is in our world.

Currently, published papers and books regarding the usefulness and implementation of the new sciences, chaos theory and complexity theory to leadership and organizational development in South Africa are almost non-existent. Research in these areas is important if we are to make meaning of the many challenges facing leaders and managers in a transformational country such as ours. Many South African organizations and their leaders are therefore called upon to change their thinking, their behaviours, and their organizations to provide a congruent experience for *all* involved in a new redesigned leadership. The traditional scientific approach to leadership promised to provide leaders with the capacity to analyse, predict and control the behaviour of the complex organizations that they lead. But, the world most leaders currently inhabit often appears to be unpredictable, uncertain, paradoxical and even uncontrollable. New science, chaos- and complexity theory, on the other hand, emphasize chaos, uncertainty, holism, patterns of behaviour, and complexity. Today scientists are developing powerful descriptions of the ways complex systems cope effectively with uncertainty and rapid change, and therein lies an opportunity for fruitful dialogue between the world of leadership and the world of science.

Today's business environment is characterized by faster technology development and information flow, increasing interconnectedness between organizations, and much greater diversity among people. These changes make it increasingly difficult for us to foresee the consequences of our actions and stay 'in control'. Many people fear that the new theories, presented in this chapter, are propagating the termination of formal leaders. On the contrary, *leaders are going to become even more critically important* because they are making a transition from hierarchical forms of organization to self-organizing, 'web-like structures'. The general idea is that leaders can profit from getting to know the dynamic behavioural states their organizations can be in, and will be able to adjust their leadership styles to the conditions of their particular state, or make efforts to change the state. In our experience, the uncertainties of potential chaos seldom cause problems; instead, it is the instinctive move to impose order on potential chaos that makes trouble for people and organizations. Leaders who intend being successful in the future will *tolerate chaos, uncertainty and lack of structure and are therefore prepared to keep answers in suspense, avoiding premature closure on important issues.* These leaders bring to bear a variety of imaginations on the growth, and development, of people and organizations, and impel others to act in ways that are truly transformational. As such, potential expands!

As we begin to step back and let go of the machine models, we begin to appreciate our wholeness. Leaders need to begin to speak a new language, and to speak in earnest of more fluid and organic structures, to begin to recognize organizations as systems, construing them as learning organizations and crediting them with some form of self-renewing capacity. Leaders need to forego the despair created by such common organizational events as change, chaos, information overload, uncertainty, and cyclical behaviours if they recognize that organizations are conscious entities, possessing many of the properties of living systems. The challenge is therefore for leaders and organizations, who are still clinging to the old metaphors, to redesign their roles and organizations far-from-equilibrium in order to honour and make use of the totality of who we are — and who others are in relation to us.

It is therefore hoped that leaders, throughout organizations, communities and families, embark on personal sense-making exercises, in order to equip themselves with a toolkit with which to engage in 'life's movement toward coherence' (Wheatley and Kellner-Rogers, 1996). Leaders have to *start asking some pertinent, critical questions* — the right questions — during this period of transition. The basic organizing question should be: 'What do we want to create?' This leads to the other fundamental question people should ask when they organize together: 'How is this world going to be different because you and I are working together?' We do not believe that these questions are being asked in all South African organizations, and in those organizations where they are being asked, we do not believe that they are being asked frequently enough. Even at a national level, they are not being asked. We should be asking, 'What is the future that we want for South Africa?' 'Who are we, and who are others, going to be in the future?' 'How can I make a difference in the country, and in people's lives?' 'What is possible right now, and what is needed?' 'Where do I start applying my talents, skills, networks, resources and energy, in order to make a difference?'

Organizations are going to have to acknowledge, at least, that what they want to create in terms of growth and profit is not necessarily what people are willing to work for, in terms of greater meaning and shared purpose. That is a lesson that is starting to creep in, and both current and future leaders need to take cognizance of that.

In conclusion, new science, chaos- and complexity theory are affecting our understanding of organizations, and therefore have serious implications for the leadership of these organizations. While many of our approaches might not change, these theories provide us with novel and alternative viewpoints to understand organizations and leadership. We have to turn on its head the way we approach 'reality'. We treated regular, orderly, predictable linear systems as if they are what is normal and regular, while in fact the sciences have shown us that they are special cases. Organizations and their leaders should therefore allow for multiple goals, embrace the concept of multiple effects and multiple causes within the framework of a matrix-like organization, and understand, with new insight, the complex interrelationship between causes and effects.

All theories and models give us only a partial view of reality. The theme of this chapter is no exception to that rule, and is not a prescription or absolute. It can be likened to a set of spectacle lenses, something through which to view organizations in order to reveal those things that give leaders more potency and personal energy, and that enable them to do things well, both now and in the future. The test of these principles is whether it adds to our understanding of organizational behaviour and can be applied to assisting leaders in managing and leading organizations. It is hoped that it leads to a whole new way of thinking about organizations and the way leaders behave, and will assist in an ongoing process of personal and organizational self-reflection, with unforeseeable outcomes. We believe firmly that new science is alerting us to the fact that, out of the increasing complexity we are experiencing in the world, simplicity in our approaches to leadership can be achieved. As Margaret Wheatley (1992) puts it:

> Hopefully, these newer sciences point the way to a simpler way to lead organizations. But to arrive at that simplicity, we will have to change our behaviours and beliefs about information, relationships, control and chaos. We will need to recognize that we live in a universe that is ordered in ways we never suspected, and by processes that are invisible except for their effects.

Complexity
Uncertainty and Change

The post-modern world can . . . be seen as one characterized by randomness and chaos, by a lack of certainty, by a plethora of competing views and voices, by complex temporalities, and where organizations are unable to produce recipes for dealing with the unstable environment. In essence, the post-modernist approach rejects the notions of . . . linearity and regular patterning. Change can occur in any direction at any time, which itself could be conceived of in new ways such as 'spiral time'.

Burrell, 1992

Both as individuals, and as members of societies, people are finding it increasingly difficult to cope with a world that is changing daily, becoming more complex and uncertain. Theorists, researchers, politicians, families, communities, business managers and leaders are all concerned about the question of how people will be able to live in an increasingly turbulent world, and what possibilities are open to them under these complex conditions. There is a widespread notion that societies, organizations and people, are generally resistant to change and uncertainty. However it may be more accurate to say that people resist being changed, especially, as is so often the case, when this happens without consultation or participation. According to Booysen and Beaty (1997: 11), resistance to change may develop from the individual, the organization, or both. Both individual and organizational resistance to change, and its sources, have been well documented in the academic literature (for example Nadler, 1983; Strebel, 1996; Carrell, Jennings and Hearin, 1997; Robbins, 1997, Greenberg and Baron, 1993). Currents of change are flowing through every domain of society, shaking the quasi-stable state. Most of human and social reality, instead of being in an orderly, stable equilibrium, is seething and bubbling with change, disorder and process (Toffler, 1981 in Merry, 1995). Although this observation was made by Toffler at the beginning of the 1980s, it is even more relevant to the human reality at the start of the twenty-first century. It might be argued that South Africa, which is 'seething and bubbling' with change, is a very apt microcosm of the global condition.

Because the external environment in which organizations operate is changing unpredictably, leadership approaches based on Taylorian principles (which involve taking apart, analysing, dividing and conquering, over-specializing, etc., regardless of how well executed) are no longer effective (Gilliland, Tynan and Smith, 1996). The high level of unpredictability in organizations, due to accelerating change and increasing complexity (for example technology, geopolitical climate, communication networks, the changing nature of work, information availability, globalization), makes Taylorian approaches to strategic planning, leadership, management and change, obsolete. South Africa is experiencing extraordinary change and transformation in all sectors of life and business. Effective change and transformation are management and leadership issues that have, and will continue to become, a way of life (Booysen and Beaty, 1997). This includes dealing with, on one hand, globalization and international competition, and on the other hand dealing with cultural diversity issues at a local level. The challenge for South Africa is in some ways more daunting than for other parts of the world. Due to anti-apartheid sanctions and international isolation, South Africa was cut off from the rest of the world for some time. This social, political and economic isolation meant that South African organizations, in particular, were not exposed to new approaches in leadership and management, and were not able to participate in exchanges of ideas. The result is that South Africa, on re-entering the global arena, inevitably has some catching up to do.

In short, for the foreseeable future, organizations and communities, both in South Africa and internationally, will be responding to an environment of perpetual change, and to a level of complexity that is not comprehensible to any one individual. This alters the fundamental nature of the leadership model and management approach that will produce success. Inevitably, this begs the question as to which leadership model will produce success? Our view is that there is not one answer to this question, as the changing environment is so complex for just one model to induce effective leadership. Nevertheless, we do consider it useful to look at some models and perspectives which have tried to clarify our understanding of what contributes to effective leadership during times of change.

Leaders of transformation

During times of change it is critical to engage the commitment of employees in the context of shared values and a shared vision. For managing change, the notion of transformational leadership is regarded as particularly relevant (Sadler, 1997). Transformational leadership is seen as a contrast to the Western paradigm of transactional leadership in which the leader and followers are regarded as very much separate entities, with separate needs. Transactional leadership occurs when managers take the initiative in offering some form of need satisfaction in return for something valued by employees, such as pay, promotion, improved job satisfaction or recognition (Sadler, 1997).

In transformational leadership, the needs of leaders and followers are regarded as more interdependent, involving relationships of mutual trust between leaders and those being led. *Our capacity to trust in others is critical to all our relationships, including those at work* — the necessary fluid glue. When we have a high capacity to trust others, we are more willing and able to work in a fluid, flexible fashion — sharing information, sharing experiences, sharing joy and pain, depending on others, empowering others, working towards getting the relationship to a higher level. According to Reina and Reina (1999: 16) 'mutual trusting relationships grow the more we share information (communication trust), keep agreements (contractual trust), and respect people's abilities (competence trust)'. In 1990, Bass and Avolio (in Sadler, 1997) suggested that transformational leadership has four components:

1. *Idealized influence.* Having a clear vision and sense of purpose. Such leaders are able to win the trust and respect of followers, by showing them they can accomplish more than they believed possible. These leaders build a base for future missions which enables them to obtain extra efforts from followers.
2. *Individual consideration.* Paying attention to the needs and potential for development of their individual followers. Delegating, coaching, mentoring and giving constructive feedback.
3. *Intellectual stimulation.* Actively soliciting new ideas and new ways of doing things.
4. *Inspiration.* Motivating people, generating enthusiasm, setting an example, being seen to share the load.

Tichy and Devanna (1986), having observed a number of transformational leaders in action, drew the conclusion that they shared a number of common characteristics that differentiated them from transactional leaders:

- They clearly see themselves as *change agents*. They set out to make a difference and to transform the organization for which they are responsible.
- They are *courageous*. They can deal with resistance, take a stand, take risks, confront reality. They are like pieces of bamboo that can be bent wildly during a storm or stampede, but are able to right themselves when calm is restored.
- They *believe in people*. They have a belief in unlimited human potential, and an optimism that goes beyond already well-developed beliefs in the importance of motivation, trust and empowerment.
- They are driven by a strong set of *values*.
- They are *life-long learners*. They view mistakes, both theirs and others', as learning opportunities.
- They are able to handle *complexity, uncertainty and ambiguity.*
- They are *visionaries*.

The distinction between transformational and transactional leadership provides a useful, initial framework from which to start thinking about the type of attributes, abilities, and characteristics of leaders during periods of change. However, it should be seen as just that: an initial framework to start the debate and discussion — a framework far more suited to thinking and research in the late 1980s than to our chaotic world at the beginning of the twenty-first century, as it places too much emphasis on the role of the leader in bringing about change, and the leader's presumed attributes. Inherent in the argument is the fact that leadership resides within one senior individual in an organization, and its focus is on the changing environment and organizational climate rather than on people and the internal and personal change processes. There are other myths of leadership such as that people are genetically predisposed to leadership; that they are charismatic; that they are at the top of the organization; that they are a rare commodity; that they are born in wealthy and well-connected families. These myths are exposed in Bennis and Goldsmith's (1994) book, *Learning to Lead: A Workbook on Becoming a Leader*, and they reinforce the perspective, which we support, that the ability to lead can be developed.

It is our belief that real change and the ability to adapt to change within organizations, in industry, and changes in the world at large, *has to start within each individual*. It has to start with their assumed ways of behaviour, their thinking paradigms and their inherent energy. Successful leaders will have to be willing to learn and constantly be aware of the way people think, how and why they behave in certain ways, how they learn and unlearn, and how to tap into their personal energy. The following sections deal with (a) the way organizations learn in times of change, (b) understanding how people unlearn and change their minds, (c) how to tap into people's energy and creativity, and (d) some guiding principles for leaders of change.

Organizational learning

Organizational learning is increasingly becoming popular in organizations that are interested in increasing competitive advantage, innovation, and effectiveness during this period of uncertainty and change at the start of the twenty-first century. Argyris and Schön (1978: 2), two of the early researchers in this field, defined organizational learning as 'the detection and correction of error'. Fiol and Lyles (1985: 803) define learning as 'the process of improving actions through better knowledge and understanding'. Dodgson (1993: 377) describes organizational learning as 'the way firms build, supplement, and organize knowledge and routines around their activities and within their cultures and adapt and develop organizational efficiency by improving the use of broad skills of their workforces'. Huber (1991: 89) states that learning occurs in an organization 'if through its processing of information, the range of its [organization's] potential behaviours is changed'. A 'learning organization' is an organization that purposefully constructs structures and strategies so as to enhance and maximize organizational learning (Dodgson, 1993). The concept of a learning organization is increasingly becoming popular, since organizations want and have to be more adaptable to change. It therefore becomes imperative, almost a responsibility, that leaders throughout, and at all levels of, organizations understand and are knowledgeable of the way in which their organizations learn, and what behaviours and processes are necessary to facilitate learning.

Goals of organizational and individual learning

Learning is a conscious attempt on the part of organizations to retain and improve competitiveness, productivity, and innovation in uncertain technological and market circumstances. The greater the uncertainties, the greater the need for learning. Organizations, and individuals, learn in order to improve their adaptability and efficiency during times of change (Dodgson, 1993). Grantham and Nichols (1993) state that learning enables quicker and more effective responses to a complex and dynamic environment. Learning also increases information sharing, communication, understanding, the levels of energy and excitement in individuals, and the quality of decisions made in organizations. Stata (1989) states that, although learning takes time, once the process has started, it feeds on itself and organizational members get better at what they do, quicker. Brown and Duguid (1986) view learning as a bridge between work and innovation/creativity.

Types of organizational learning

Argyris and Schön (1978) describe three types of organizational learning:

1. *Single-loop learning (SLL):* Organizational learning occurs when errors are detected and corrected, and companies carry on with their present policies and goals. According to Dodgson (1993), SLL can be equated to activities that add to the knowledge base or company-specific competencies or routines without altering the fundamental nature of the organizational activities. SLL has also been referred to as 'adaptive learning' or 'coping' by Senge (1990a).

2. *Double-loop learning (DLL):* DLL occurs when, in addition to detection and correction of errors, the organization is involved in the questioning and modification of existing norms, procedures, policies, and objectives. DLL involves changing the organization's knowledge base or company-specific competencies or routines (Dodgson, 1993). DLL is also called 'generative learning', or 'learning to expand an organization's capabilities' by Senge (1990a).

3. *Deutero learning (DL):* Deutero learning occurs when organizations learn how to carry out single-loop and double-loop learning. The first two forms of learning will not occur if the organizations are not aware that learning must occur. Awareness of ignorance motivates learning (Brown and Duguid, 1986). This means identifying the learning orientations or styles, and the processes and structures (facilitating factors) required to promote learning. Double-loop and deutero learning are concerned with the 'why' and 'how' to change the organization, while single-loop learning is concerned with 'accepting change without questioning underlying assumptions and core beliefs'. The type of organizational learning also depends on where in the organization learning occurs. Thus, learning can occur in different functions, and at different levels, of the organization such as research and development, design, engineering, manufacturing, marketing, administration, and sales.

Another way of looking at learning in a personal sense, is through the concepts of unconscious incompetence (I don't know what I don't know; blissful ignorance) and conscious incompetence (I am aware of my incompetence 'the stage when a person confronts how much they do not know; the sense of hitting rock bottom' — Vint, Recaldin and Gould, 1998: 207). If *unconscious incompetence* exists, you cannot learn. Through humility you can become aware of your incompetence (*conscious incompetence*) at which point you begin to learn and grow in confidence, which gets you to *conscious competence* (I can do this, and I am very aware of the skills involved) to *unconscious competence* (I can do it without thinking about it). Here, the individual sets himself, or herself, up for a 'win' with more practical action plans, having reviewed thoroughly what did not work previously and for what reasons (1998: 208). Things then start to go right for the individual who begins to get results. This is reinforced by feedback from others who tell him or her that, not only is she or he getting it right, but other people agree with him or her, start to accept his or her ideas and initiate change themselves.

Learning is a dynamic concept and it emphasizes the continually changing nature of organizations and individuals. Just as learning is essential for the growth of individuals, it is equally important for organizations. Jack Welch, CEO of General Electric in the US, made the following statement regarding learning at General Electric: 'Our behaviour is driven by a fundamental core belief: The desire, and the ability of an organization to continuously learn from any source — and to rapidly convert this learning into action — is its ultimate competitive advantage' (Welch, 1996). Since individuals form the core of the organization, they must establish the necessary norms and processes to enable organizational learning, in order to facilitate change. Organizational learning is more than the sum of the parts of individual learning. An organization does not lose out on its learning abilities when members leave the organization. This is true of organizations in which learning is well-embedded within, and integrated into, its culture. Organizational memory plays a very critical role in organizational learning. Both the demonstrability and usability of learning depend on the effectiveness of the organizational memory (Huber, 1991). Organizational memory refers to the repository where knowledge is stored for future use. It is also called 'corporate knowledge' or 'corporate genetics' by Hamel and Prahalad (1994). Decision makers store and retrieve not only hard data or information, but also 'soft' information, that is, information with meaning. This soft or interpreted information can be in the form of tacit know-how, expertise, biases, experiences, lists of contacts, anecdotes, stories, metaphors, and so on. The major challenge for leaders and their organizations exists in interpreting information and creating organizational memory that is easily accessible. Some organizations opt to pool all their ideas, thoughts, processes, etc., on an internal Intranet — and this will serve as a future 'collective memory' for the organization. Researchers such as Dodgson (1993), Brown and Duguid (1986) merely make a passing mention of the influence of technology on learning. They suggest that new technologies such as multimedia communications, computer-aided learning, information dissemination and training will be a great ground for future research in this area. Technology can be used to clarify assumptions, speed up communications, elicit tacit knowledge, and construct histories of insights and catalogue them. Technology has the potential to eliminate barriers to learning in three key ways. Firstly, by flattening the structure of the organization and shifting the locus of control. Secondly, by allowing easy and timely dissemination of information to all employees, and thus making the organization more informed (but not necessarily more organic or flexible!), and thirdly, by making knowledge an accessible resource. The three ways form the basis for what is now termed 'knowledge management'.

Organizational learning contributes to organizational memory. Thus, learning systems not only influence immediate members, but also future members due to the accumulation of histories, experiences, norms, and stories. Peter Senge (1990a), who popularized 'learning organizations' in his book *The Fifth Discipline: The Art and Practice of the Learning Organization*, described them as places 'where people continually expand their capacity to create the results they truly desire, where new and expansive patterns of thinking are nurtured, where collective aspiration is set free, and where people are continually learning how to learn together'. To achieve these ends, Senge suggested the use of 'five component technologies': systems thinking, personal mastery, mental models, shared vision, and team learning.

For those unfamiliar with Senge's work, it may be useful to look briefly at what these technologies involve. Firstly, *systems thinking*, like the new sciences and chaos theory, is a discipline for seeing wholes — for seeing patterns of relationships, rather than seeing incidents, events or things in isolation. Hence, for example, Senge would argue that today's problems come from yesterday's solutions — everything is connected. The second technology, *personal mastery*, essentially refers to the fact that organizations can only learn if the individuals within the organizations learn. Personal mastery thus embodies the concept of personal growth, of expanding one's personal ability. *Mental models* as touched on in the chapter on awareness, are deep-seated notions and assumptions, sometimes unknown to ourselves, that influence our perceptions and behaviour. They need to be surfaced, challenged and their influences need to be understood. *Shared visions* emerge from personal visions, and therefore the concept of personal mastery is important to shared vision as well. Senge argues that, if genuinely shared, vision provides purpose and energy to people and breeds excellence and learning in organizations. The fifth technology, *team learning*, is in essence a process of aligning teams to prevent wasting energy and to ensure the creation of the results the team desires. True team learning needs to begin with dialogue in which members suspend assumptions and think together, a concept that is explored further in the chapter on communication.

In 1999, Senge et al. further explored the 'five component technologies' and defined 'learning capabilities' as 'skills and proficiencies that, among individuals, teams, and larger communities, enable people to consistently enhance their capacity to produce results that are truly important to them' (Senge et al., 1999: 45). In other words, learning capabilities enable us to learn. Senge and his co-authors continue to see the five learning disciplines of *The Fifth Discipline* as a foundation for every organization, no matter how large or small, because the capabilities they nurture support so many other capabilities:

- *aspiration:* the capability to orient, individually and collectively toward creating what people truly desire, rather than just reacting to circumstances (based on personal mastery and building shared vision);
- *reflective conversation:* the capability to converse in ways that nurture reflection and inquiry, to build shared understanding, and to coordinate reflective action (based on mental models and team learning); and
- *understanding complexity:* the capability to see patterns of interdependency underlying problems, and to distinguish short-term from long-term consequences of actions (based on systems thinking).

The work of Senge and his co-authors may be regarded as a seminal work in the field of leadership, and consequently many subsequent writings on leadership have focused, either individually or collectively, on the five component technologies. For leaders, and potential leaders, this signals the importance of learning. Nonaka (1991: 97) characterizes knowledge-creating companies as places where 'inventing new knowledge is not a specialized activity . . . it is a way of behaving, indeed, a way of being, in which *everyone* is a knowledge worker'. Nonaka and Takeuchi (1995) suggest that companies use metaphors and organizational redundancy to focus thinking, encourage dialogue, and make tacit, instinctively understood ideas explicit.

Watkins and Marsick (1993) researched large American companies that have made collective learning central to their work ethos, and found that these companies share a number of features. The companies tended to have the following:

- leaders who model calculated risk-taking and experimentation;
- decentralized decision making and employee empowerment;
- skill inventories and audits of learning capacity;
- systems for sharing learning and using it in the business;
- rewards and structures for employee initiative;
- consideration of long-term consequences and impact on the work of others;
- frequent use of cross-functional teams;
- opportunities to learn from experience on a daily basis;
- a culture of feedback and disclosure.

A key part of the creation of a learning culture within a business is the education of all employees about the fundamentals of doing business. This includes full access to information that generates the bottom line: the cost of doing business, and the profits that result and how they are being spent. This is called *open-book management* and has really been adopted only by smaller, idealistic and egalitarian companies in the US, but with great success as workers can monitor the effect of their increased productivity on the bottom line and their own pay. They are thus also encouraged to feel greater responsibility for the company's financial health and, by extension, their own job security. The trade union movement in South Africa has made repeated calls for a similar approach to management to be adopted in all enterprises in South Africa. Thus far, calls for legislation to this effect have been resisted. The open-book management approach is in line with Wheatley's interpretation of the new sciences in which she sees information as the lifeblood of the organization, and the more information that is shared, the better.

To summarize, organizational learning occurs due to the interplay of various factors such as structure, the people, the context, strategy, environment, technology, and culture. More and more organizations have realized that, in order to be successful in a highly competitive, changing and unpredictable environment, they must encourage double-loop and deutero learning. The implications of not becoming a learning organization can be costly (Grantham and Nichols, 1993). Grantham states that 'it will result in loss of market share, loss of competitive edge, loss of intangibles such as reputation, loss of energized staff, and loss of the ability to attract only the best and brightest'. It is no wonder, therefore, that forward-thinking companies in South Africa, such as the Liberty Group, have recently placed enormous emphasis on information flow, learning and people development. It is no longer sufficient, in the financial services sector, for organizations to be doing those things that have made them successful in the past. The American automobile industry is another good example of this. It was initially caught sleeping at the wheel by the Japanese automobile manufacturers who overtook an industry that was complacent and arrogant, with a belief that it had nothing to learn. We witness the same pattern of events in the British automobile industry — now virtually run by the Germans. 'Learn or burn' is the slogan for twenty-first-century organizations.

Also, briefly mentioned, was how information systems can facilitate this learning process. We believe that this will be a growing trend in businesses, as more and more of them move toward 'cyber-communities', 'e-business', 'k-commerce', and 'm-commerce'. During this new century, we have got to share information as the primary organizing force in any organization. With the displacement of people due to downsizing efforts, organizations are discharging vast amounts of organizational knowledge without realizing the long-term implications of such short-term actions. One way in which organizations can preserve that knowledge and further promote organizational learning, is by using information systems to store and retrieve such collective knowledge and create corporate memories. Another is the way in which organizations, through the use of technology, can tap into knowledge resources outside the traditional organization.

The leadership and management challenges in building 'learning organizations' represent a microcosm of the central leadership issue of our times: how communities, be they corporate or civil societies, productively confront complex, systemic issues where hierarchical authority is inadequate for change. 'None of today's most pressing issues will be resolved through hierarchical authority' (Senge et al., 1995: 19). Some things are very sure: there are no simple causes, no simple fixes; there is no one villain to blame; there will be no magic pill. *Significant change will require imagination, perseverance, dialogue, deep caring, and a willingness to change on the part of many people.* The challenges of systemic change where hierarchy is ineffectual will, we believe, push us to new views of leadership and management, based on new principles. These challenges cannot be met by isolated heroic leaders. They will require a unique mix of different people, in different positions, who lead and learn in different ways — and therefore changes will be required in our traditional leadership and management models.

Rethinking and de-engineering our thinking

Over the years, there has been a great deal written about individual and organizational learning (for example Shrivastava, 1983; Fiol and Lyles, 1985; Levitt and March, 1988; Senge, 1996; 1994; 1990a; 1990b; Brown and Duguid, 1986; Huber, 1991; Grantham, 1993; Dodgson, 1993). According to Hamel and Prahalad (1994), creating a learning organization is only half the solution to a challenging problem. Equally important is the creation of an 'unlearning organization', which essentially means that the organization, and the individual, must forget some of its past. A small amount has been written about unlearning (for example Starbuck and Hedberg, 1977; Argyris and Schön, 1978; Hedberg, 1981; Nystrom and Starbuck, 1984), but the concept has been dwindling from the academic literature. However, new efforts to revitalize and inform people has surfaced again (for example Wheatley, 1999; Bettis and Prahalad, 1995; Farr, 1995). Bettis and Prahalad (1995: 10) make the point that, during periods of organizational uncertainty and change, the organization wishing to be successful in the future must 'unlearn the old logic . . . the focus shifts from learning to unlearning in the case of strategic change'. They argue that fundamental change will take place only through the *gradual unlearning of the existing dominant logic*, which will be brought about by the deliberate construction of important organizational events that will decrease stability and challenge the existing dominant logic. However, the authors further assert that strategic learning and unlearning are inextricably intertwined. Our sense is that a new kind of learning needs to take place, both within individuals and organizations, whilst simultaneously unlearning obsolete practices and behaviours, mindsets, and skill-sets.

Wheatley (1992) makes the point that we are not comfortable with chaos [and uncertainty], even in our thoughts, and we want to move out of confusion as quickly as possible. This seems to be part of the human condition. Another quote made famous by Wheatley, is from Burt Mannis who, in *The Leader's Edge*, said: 'In this day and age, if you're not confused, you're not thinking clearly.' We know that our old thoughts are not going to get us into the future that we desire, so confusion is the only alternative for a while. The other thing is that people are already confused, so to hear that it can be a healthy stage gives people a lot of comfort. It is not healthy if you stay in it your whole life, but it can be healthy if it is part of your process of moving on, of letting things reconfigure. It is our view that talking about chaos theory in that way, and understanding that confusion may be part of a much deeper process of organization, is a good thing.

People at all levels in organizations, within communities and families, really have to 'de-engineer' their thinking, which means that they have to examine how mechanistically they are oriented, even in their treatment of one another. People need to feel free and not afraid when reflecting, testing possibilities and outcomes, and evaluating past actions and decisions. This is especially true in organizations. Currently, however, it is believed that we can best lead and manage people by making assumptions more fitting to machines than people. So we assume that, like good machines, people have no desire, no heart, no spirit, no compassion, no real intelligence — because machines do not have any of that. The great dream of machines is that you give them a set of instructions, and they will follow it. We see the history of leadership and management as an effort to perfect the instructions that you hope someone will follow this time — even though they have never followed directions in their whole life.

> When you try to change an organization, you try to get people to change their behaviors. Since behavior is controlled by the mind, the only way to get the change you want is to change people's minds. And since the only one who can change a person's mind is that person, the only way you can get the change you want is to get people to change their own minds.

Farr, 1995: 5

Failure to understand this fact leads to one of the most common errors leaders make in managing change, that is, they act on the assumption that they can change someone else's mind. Farr continues by claiming that once, through our experience, we settle on programs (in the mind) that work, we tend to automate them. Chris Argyris (1999) refers to these as 'theories of action', programs in our heads, functioning like software that regulates how we deal with future situations. This saves energy and frees our consciousness to do things other than make conscious choices among routine actions. These mindsets then act as filters that create our perceptions, which in turn trigger the programs that control our actions. Neale Donald Walsch tells us:

> Every action taken by human beings is based in love and fear, not simply those dealing with relationships. Decisions affecting business, industry, politics, religion, the education of our young, the social agenda of our nations, the economic goals of our society, choices involving war, peace, attack, defence, aggression, submission; determinations to covet or give away, to save or to share, to unite or to divide — every single free choice we ever undertake arises out of one of the only two possible thoughts there are: a thought of love or a thought of fear.

Walsch, 1997: 18–19

As is shown in Figure 4.1, the Walsch principles illustrate the generation of 'pictures' (mindsets) in people: 'what I see' leads to two possible courses of action, that is, an action resulting from a fear reaction, or an action resulting from a love reaction. From a fear action, negative energy is generated (the individual is drained of energy), and from a love action, positive action is generated (the individual's energy increases). Either of the two reactions lead to 'what I do', which results in 'what I get'. This process of 'see', 'do' and 'get' was first articulated by Stephen Covey in *The Seven Habits of Highly Effective People* (1989). As we settle into these mindsets, we automatically and unconsciously begin to rely upon them as our ego's basis for safety, survival, and satisfaction. Thus, we create one of the foundations of ego — the automatic function of mind to 'be right'. To violate those mindsets comes to be unconsciously experienced as 'wrong', which threatens ego with fear, which we automatically and unconsciously seek to avoid. The result of all of this is a universal tendency to resist being changed, and to stick to what our mindsets tell us to see and do. We have been taught to live in fear. We have been told about the survival of the fittest and the victory of the strongest and the success of the cleverest (Walsch, 1997). So we strive to be the fittest, the strongest, the cleverest — in one way or another — and if we see ourselves as anything less than this in any situation, we fear loss, for we have been told that to be less is to lose. Farr (1995: 5) suggests the following guideline for leaders: 'When you want to change something in operations and processes that requires a change in old behaviour patterns of people, use tactics that get people to examine and decide to change their own mindsets to what the new behaviours require.'

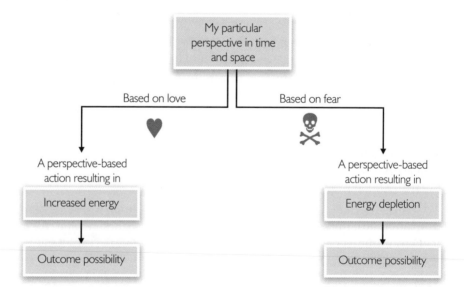

Figure 4.1
An interpretation of the Walsch principles

Robert Haas, Chairman and CEO of Levi Strauss & Co., observes:

> Change isn't easy. It's difficult to unlearn behaviors that made us successful in the past. Speaking rather than listening. Valuing people like yourself over people of different genders and cultures. Doing things on your own rather than collaborating. Making the decision yourself instead of asking different people for their perspectives. There's a whole range of behaviors that were highly functional in the old hierarchy that are dead wrong in flatter, more responsive, empowered organizations.
>
> *Robert Haas in Bennis, 1996: 16*

When we speak about 'de-engineering', we want you, the reader, to realize that the bottom line is that *we are alive, we are human beings*. We possess all the attributes that somehow disappeared in the mechanistic way of thinking. At the organizational level, the same is true. You cannot just give an organization of people a set of directions, a re-engineered business process, a new organizational chart, a new boss, a new set of behavioural expectations — you cannot just legislate that, because it does not happen. Yet corporations are, during this time of the re-engineering frenzy, spending sums of money that literally go into the millions on developing new engineering plans for the organization. Wheatley, in an interview with Richard Katz (1997: 19–20), stated that she prefers to talk about 'de-engineering' rather than re-engineering. She claims that the 70–80 % failure rate of re-engineering efforts was totally predictable. 'Whenever you are taking an engineering approach to human organizations, you are going to get an enormous amount of backlash, resistance and bitterness, because people have not been included.' Before putting forth ideas and demands, leaders should map the mental terrain, both within themselves and others, to find out what the current mindsets are. Once existing mindsets are known, then leadership actions can be developed that will challenge them, and will encourage people to create new mindsets that respond positively to leadership requests for new actions to create change.

At the edge of energy

Many people intuitively feel that too much chaos, unpredictability and uncertainty is problematic for regular healthy organizational functioning, but they have greater difficulty understanding why too much order can also be unhealthy. Managing is often seen as creating and maintaining order in an organization so as to ensure the regular, orderly, sequential and undisturbed work flow. The problem is not in the organization functioning in an orderly way, the difficulties arise when the organization attempts to be so orderly that it excludes the chaotic elements of novelty, discontinuous change, innovation, experimentation, development, entrepreneurship, self-organization and creativity. Too much order can be dysfunctional in systems that need to adapt to changing circumstances, and especially the conditions of burgeoning uncertainty of our times.

An exactly regular heartbeat, for instance, can be the sign of a coming heart attack. A healthy heartbeat has elements of irregularity. When brainwaves are very orderly they may signify an epileptic fit. Brainwaves during creative activity show chaotic patterns. Too much order and regularity means that everything is fixed and can be predicted and the system is not able to adapt to changing environmental conditions. There is no place left for change, variety, creativity, emergence and novelty, which are essential for functioning under changing circumstances. A butterfly that flies in a straight line without unexpected zigzags will become easy prey. Too much order and regularity in an organization means that everything is fixed, frozen and predictable, leaving the organization no leeway to manoeuvre itself — it cannot be adaptive or flexible in this way. Every organization which functions in a turbulent environment needs transformative change, new behavioural choices, fresh directions, novel strategies, innovative work processes, changing organizational structures, new norms and rules and rich, messy communication channels. Without these the organization will not survive.

Ralph Stacey, director of the Complexity and Management Centre at the University of Hertfordshire (UK), believes that an area of bounded stability exists in the chaos where the introduction of new concepts and ideas can result in highly accelerated results. Stacey suggests that leaders must look beyond the constraints of order, into the area of 'bounded chaos' for strategic solutions. 'Intuitively, the patterns we observe all point to the importance of chaos in the practice of business leadership. The failure to predict . . . provides further intuitive support' (Stacey, 1991: 361). During a lecture on complexity theory, Stacey related the following story: 'Suppose there is a big city of 10 million people who have to be fed and there needs to be a system of how to feed them and at the same time build up a two weeks' inventory for these people' (Tidhult, 1997). Stacey explained that 'the problem will take care of itself, the people will be fed because the markets are self-organizing. It is a complex adaptive system, a network system responding in a non-linear system (for every action I make there could be many responses). No local government has said what should be done, the system is producing it. No one can understand the system, no one is in control of it' (Tidhult, 1997). Jeffrey Goldstein, in his 1994 book, *The Unshackled Organization*, says that 'self-organization is a self-guiding process. This means that change is neither a hierarchically controlled nor an externally driven process . . . self-organization represents a system undergoing a revolution prompted by far-from-equilibrium conditions.'

Figure 4.2 has been adapted from a summary of a lecture given by Ralph Stacey at the Skandia Future Center's 1997 Lecture Series. Stacey posed the following questions, and then proposed a model:

- What are the basic situations in which we have to operate?
- There are two very simple fundamental key factors that have to do with the degree of certainty in joined action:
    - How far from certainty are we when we have to act?
    - How far from agreement are we?
        1. Close to certainty = We are able to predict, to forecast, to plan

2. Far from certainty = We are unable to identify the link between cause and effect, we are far from grasping the future through long range planning
3. We are close to agreement as a group = We share the same objectives, purposes, goals
4. We are far from agreement = We have different objectives, purposes, goals

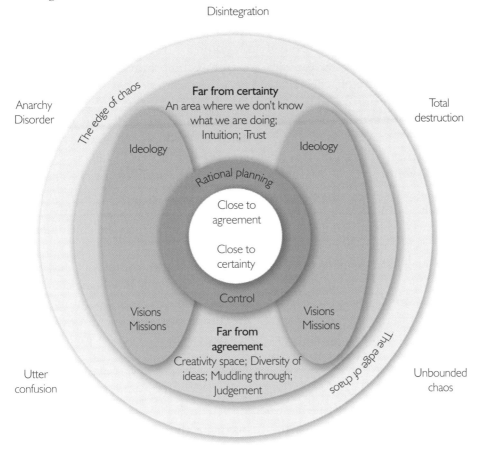

Figure 4.2
An interpretation of Ralph Stacey's 'bounded chaos'

If we cannot predict the outcome, we cannot make long-term plans or sometimes do not have confidence to proceed. *High trust in stretching* into uncertainty becomes critical.

> In reality, success for an organization does not depend on choosing stable equilibrium over explosive instability, it emerges from a third condition that can be called bounded instability. Between the stable and unstable zones is the phase transition, the space for creativity. It has a stable legitimate system consisting of clear hierarchical structures and bureaucracies, on the one hand, and a 'shadow system', on the other hand, that is characterized by excitement, fear, tension, anxiety.
>
> *Ralph Stacey, 1992*

Computer simulations of complex adaptive networks demonstrate that it is possible for the order of new survival strategies to emerge from disorder through a process of spontaneous self-organization. Levy (1994: 168), for example, has used a non-linear simulation of international supply chains to demonstrate that managers might underestimate the costs of international production — resulting in disruptions and volatility in the production function. Levy also demonstrated that managers should be able to control the process and shift the system back into a stable state. Levy's paper represents one of the first attempts to model chaotic systems in a business management environment.

The tendency to move towards 'far-from-equilibrium conditions' may differ between cultures. Hofstede (1980, 1997), for example, has as one of his four dimensions of cultural differences, the dimension of uncertainty avoidance. According to Hofstede, the Anglophone cultures are generally low on the uncertainty avoidance scale, which means that risk-taking is encouraged. In contrast, other cultures are high on this scale, so the exhortations to take risks are interpreted very differently. A Masai friend of one of the authors, for example, advises us that 'if you pour the water too fast, the vessel will break'. The multicultural nature of South African society means that in Stacey's model, the drivers to different parts of bounded chaos within an organization may be culturally based, raising the complexity of leadership responsibility.

Complex systems have three inherent phases: order, complexity and chaos — predictability being characteristic of order and unpredictability being characteristic of chaos. Complexity is the 'edge of chaos' — the buffer zone separating order and stability from disorder and chaos. In the complexity zone one can expect to find both chaos and order. Within the complex pattern itself, leaders should try to steer their organizations to what is termed the 'edge of chaos'. Functioning at the edge of chaos is typical of adaptive systems that display sustainability. Sustainability means long-term adaptive capability under changing conditions, and entails the capacity to co-evolve with surrounding systems.

Complex adaptive systems try to navigate their functioning to the edge of chaos. This is where life has enough stability to maintain itself and enough creativity to be called life; it is where the system's components do not degenerate into stability and do not disintegrate into chaos; it is the battlefield between degeneration and anarchy. Adaptive systems try to guide their behaviour so as to function at the edge of chaos. They have to be careful, on one hand, not to degenerate into functioning in a way that is too orderly; which will lead to stagnation. On the other hand, they may fall into a turbulent, disorderly, uncertain pattern as in deep chaos, and lose their ability to function, maintain continuity, capability to absorb information and learn from experience. When a system balances itself within the complex pattern of behaviour so as to ensure its sustainability, it is at the edge of chaos. The evolutionary process is an expression of the growing capability of adaptive systems to *learn how to navigate their behaviour so that they maintain themselves at the edge of chaos*. The space for creativity in an organization lies at the edge of organizational disintegration or anarchy. The members, or agents, of a complex adaptive system in an enterprise differ from other classes of complex adaptive systems, such as flocks of birds, populations of fish, ants, and so on. The members of such an organization are human beings with all different kinds of talents, such as creativity, individualism, leadership, observer capability, and so forth. Out of the stable zone, at the edge of instability, or at the edge of chaos — it is only there that you will find variety, creativity and beauty. René de Wet, director of the very successful South African retail company, Pick 'n Pay, feels that 'conflict [at the edge of chaos] is vital to release creativity . . . and as a leader you must be seen to encourage it to release creative energies and allow free expression' (April, 1997).

There is a growing body of evidence in physics and biology too, that complex systems tend to evolve to a state of complexity at the 'edge of chaos'. Studies on phenomena as disparate as sandpiles, earthquakes and artificial life have found that systems move towards complexity. Complex behaviour enables entities in the system to maximize the benefits of stability while retaining a capacity to change. In terms of the new sciences, a state is characterized by the dominance of a specific attractor. This means that the behaviour of the organization is attracted to a specific pattern of behaviour. The attractors differ among themselves in terms of the mix of order and disorder. With the help of the different attractors, it is possible to characterize the behaviour of all complex systems. Behaviour under the sway of strange attractors *enlarges the degrees of freedom in human choice*, but also increases the measure of uncertainty and difficulty to predict behaviour, to plan and control it. This is a chaotic pattern of behaviour, in the sense of the difficulty to predict individual behaviour. While the behaviour is determined by various causes and is deterministic, it is also chaotic because it *cannot be predicted in the long term*. Behaviour in this state takes the form of the strange attractor whose gyrating irregular twists give it the name of 'strange'.

The overall behaviour does have a pattern that, throughout time, can be identified, and the form does have boundaries that set limits to behaviour, but specific concrete behaviour at a point in time cannot be predicted. It is possible to identify the outline of the pattern that serves as the framework of the dynamics of the behaviour throughout time. Behaviours do not break through the basin of attraction to which they belong. Much of organizational behaviour and relationships is based on a chaotic pattern of strange attractors, in the sense of blending a measure of macro-order with uncertainty and unpredictability of specific microbehaviours. Leaders can know that a major transformation is going to take place in the organization, but it is impossible to foretell how exactly it will affect their teams and work.

At first glance chaotic behaviour appears to be the antithesis of organizational behaviour, that necessitates order, regularity and predictability so as to ensure coordination, planning and control. A second look will remind us that variety and irregularity allow the resilience and creativity which are a necessity for learning

— which is a necessary condition to be able to survive. To function in a changing environment, adaptive teams and organizations must have the capability to change and vary their behaviours according to changing circumstances. One fixed and unchangeable uniform custom or tradition, or regulation does not allow adaptability to changing conditions. The regular heartbeat functions chaotically so as to grant elasticity and resilience in the use of different amounts of oxygen under different conditions.

One of the conditions of being able to adapt to a dynamic turbulent environment is to *match the environmental variety with internal non-linear variety*. Organizations, functioning in an agitated environment, need ever-increasing measures of novelty, creativity, change and variety. A South African example is the telecommunications company, MTN, who, along with knowledge management expert, Karl-Eric Sveiby, has developed a unique intangible assets monitor as a tool for tracking and valuing their intangible assets. Championed by the head of human resources, Paul Norman, MTN has, for the last year, systematically put in place a number of knowledge management strategies and initiatives that will indisputably give MTN the advantage of being one of the first companies in South Africa to adopt and experiment with a knowledge management culture. Paul Norman claims that the reasons why knowledge management has been identified as appropriate for MTN, include the fast growth of the company, rapid changes in the industry, a shortage of skilled resources, the need to learn fast, and a highly mobile workforce. According to the MTN Corporate Survey (1999), the intangible assets have been categorized into three different areas, and include the competencies of the staff, the external relations such as those with customers and suppliers, and the internal processes. Other activities that have been planned include joint workshops with employees, customers and suppliers, where shared visions and values are discussed. To better understand their customer, plans are under way for interpreting and analysing customer data in order to provide better customer profiling information. In the competency domain, Paul Norman lists better recruitment, management of the different stages of employees, competence mapping and a new mentor and coaching system to drive up the intangible asset of employee competence. Recognition of achievement and senior management support are considered crucial for the success of this initiative at MTN. Organizational sustainability — which is long-term survival and evolution — is not possible in a climate of turbulence if an organization clings to its old and trusted ways of functioning. Changeability becomes ever more essential as the organization's environment transforms at an ever increasing rate and evolves into forms of growing complexity. Colin Hall, executive chairman of the South African retail group, Wooltru, can be regarded in some ways as the Jack Welch (CEO of General Electric in the US) of South African business, as he is passionate about teaching leadership. Hall runs cross-sectoral leadership programmes once a month in South Africa, and in 1999, at one such programme, he commented: 'Science is helping me understand, among many things, the uses of chaos and its role in self-organization. I think I not only expect chaos now, but I've grown more trusting of it as a necessary stage to greater organization.'

Strategists, engineers, as well as systems thinkers claim that successful systems are said to be driven by negative feedback processes toward predictable states of adaptation to the environment. Complexity is concerned with the dynamic properties of non-linear network feedback systems which, when applied to ecological selection, explain how populations avoid extinction by developing *new logic*. Positive feedback systems highlight the futility of returning back to equilibrium and instead pre-empt destruction through self reinforcement and the development of a new method of responding to information, breaking the paradigm and allowing a new logic to emerge (Bettis and Prahalad, 1995: 11).

How should a leader behave when his or her organization is functioning in a complex pattern, which combines order and disorder, certainty and uncertainty, continuity and novelty? She or he can navigate the organization to function at the edge of chaos — it therefore requires courage, trust from followers, and being in tune with what people's needs and dreams are. On one side lies the danger of too much order, continuity, regularity, similarity, maintaining what is, loyalty to the past, etc. This condition stifles the energy, the creativity and the novelty-developing ability of the organization, and its people. In everyday life this takes the form of a stiff, autocratic, centralized, hierarchic managerial style; a rigid organizational structure of regulations and procedures that are prescribed in detail in all areas of functioning; uniformity in the makeup of the human population of the organization; lack of autonomy for individuals, teams, departments, etc. in the performance of their tasks. A sure way to stifle creativity and initiative!

On the other hand, there is the danger of falling into the abyss of too much disorder, of ineffectiveness stemming from exaggerated irregularity, uncertainty and instability. This is a scenario of growing chaos and uncertainty that adversely affect the functioning and sustainability of the organization. An organization can find itself in this state as a result of bad leadership that is incapable of developing basic frameworks that ensure safety and 'stability'. This may happen when the organization has forfeited its vision, and therefore its identity and people are lost in the mist of uncertainty concerning the future of the organization, and more importantly, their future in it. Organizations often enter a state of too much chaos at a certain stage in the working through of a crisis. This is a transition state during which that which had worked in the past is no longer relevant, but no new way of escaping from the maze is apparent. Bridges (1980) wrote that a transition state is one in which we are suspended in the air, much like a diver after leaving the diving platform and before touching the water. This is a period of anxiety but also a neutral period during which we have no idea whether the change will work. This sequence contrasts with the more common view on 'change projects' according to which we announce the beginning, go through the transitional phase and then expect to end the change project. In both patterns discussed above, the too orderly and the too chaotic, the organization has difficulty adapting because organizational learning is adversely affected.

An example of how chaos can adversely affect learning can be seen through an exercise that one of the authors uses in leadership training. Four people stand in the middle of a room. They are encircled by an elastic band. Each person in the group has a piece of paper indicating the task. Person 1's task is to go to the south corner of the room; person 2 to the north corner, person 3 to get person 1 and 2 to the east corner and person 4 has to go to yet another corner. The elastic is already taut. The tendency of the people is immediately to comply with the task, without questioning. Naturally the elastic stretches to a point where no one can even get close to where they want to go. Never has a group considered checking the tasks first to see if they could do them in order. These are entirely *self-imposed limits* and an illustration of how a supposedly chaotic situation can impair the planning and learning within a group.

Change and quantum leadership

Michael Quigley (1997), director of the Center for Collaborative Leadership at Rivier College (Nashua, New Hampshire, USA), claims that future organizations wanting to be successful in an environment of change and uncertainty ('quantum organizations'), will require 'quantum leaders' at all levels of the organization — both organizational and personal/individual leadership. He further claims that these effective leaders of the new quantum organizations will be recognized by the following distinct characteristics, which we feel are useful:

1. *Quantum leaders are forever looking for new ways in which the core competencies can interact more effectively to make more creativity possible.* The living, creative organization is not the same as the one on the organizational chart, which only tells us how the functions are arranged. An innovation cannot be planned in a linear or logical manner. Leaders do not expect results on demand, but rather they create the interactive processes by which improved performance can be realized. These processes are themselves forever subject to improvement. Quantum leaders allow people to work with others to generate dynamic performance and positive interaction. Personality, character, enthusiasm, and a desire to learn are as important as the possession of functional skills. In this sense, as is the case at MTN, hiring philosophies and policies are as important as training programmes.

2. *Quantum leaders ensure that the system has a sense of direction, an aim and a purpose, as well as a plan of action.* Devoid of this direction, the components of the system will fall apart. The energy of the components will be compelled to turn on the system itself and self-destruct or at least sub-optimize its capability. Leaders must ensure that the available energy is channeled in a purposeful and positive manner to achieve the aim of the organization.

3. *Quantum leadership is about the creation of energy, not controlling inertia and avoiding entropy.* Continual education (not simply skills training) is essential for increasing the intellectual power and energy of the quantum organization. New theories of learning, our multiple of intelligences, of left- and right-brain development, thinking beyond the boundaries of specialization, and under-standing the connectedness of all disciplines, is essential for development.

4. *Quantum leaders reject the philosophy of materialistic determinism and accept the 'invisible' realities of mind, soul and heart.* The quantum organization cannot be based on a philosophy of materialistic determinism. What is required is a phi-losophy that recognizes the innate value, dignity and talent of every person. Without a corporate culture that sustains human value and dignity, innova-tion and the risks involved in achieving new thinking will never materialize. Where there is fear, anxiety or humiliation, no one will take a risk on a new idea. Any system is only as strong as its weakest point.

5. *Quantum leaders are liberally educated persons.* They understand ancient truths concerning human nature. They look to the future and employ statistical methods embedded in quantum theory, that is, patterns and phase-space dia-grams, to anticipate the future. They integrate qualitative concepts with quan-titative methods, and they possess the wisdom of knowing when to use these methods. They are wise enough to know when not to use these quantitative methods. They understand the fallacy of trying to quantify human endeavour through artificial appraisal and evaluation systems. Quantum leaders under-stand that they are in the business of human development, no matter what products or services they provide.

6. *Quantum leadership entails facilitating and enabling components to interact in new ways.* Any attempt to dictate arbitrary outputs from the components will ul-timately result in failure of the entire system, for to do so ignores random variations present within the system, and suppresses the personal freedom from which the output originates.

7. *Quantum leaders must be servant-leaders who understand, both intuitively and formally, the available talent of associates.* Such leaders operate as respected coaches and mentors in leading everyone to achieve the purpose of the system. The competition, the quantum system finds itself involved in, is its own pre-vious performance, which it seeks to improve. For this to happen, it must rely on its own capabilities, not on comparing itself with the performance of others.

8. *Quantum leaders understand that satisfaction in one's work ought to be both in-trinsic and extrinsic.* Any organization, as well as people, requires external re-sources to survive, but more important are the intrinsic criteria for learning, innovation and being. Quantum leaders seek to balance both realities through personnel policies and education.

9. *Quantum leaders understand that the positive interaction of human forces is built on a foundation of 'invisible energy', namely spiritual and moral principles.* Freedom without inherent order results in scattered, wasted energy, as does order without freedom. This moral energy is the deep personal integrity of the leader and associates, the trust this generates in the organization, and the resulting harmony that enables everyone to be courageous in the quest for knowledge and innovation. Freedom is the basis for opportunity; it develops a moral order in shaping personal responsibilities toward achieving the greater good of the whole, in which the good of the individual is to be found. In this shared moral universe, economic, political and social entities, which interact with other larger systems, give rise to greater human achievement.

10. *The leader of the quantum system is a person of spiritual and moral integrity, who develops a clear vision and sense of purpose.* The leader inspires others to follow through their free commitment and ownership of the vision. The leader ensures that a plan exists which will enable associates to achieve their greatest personal development, in seeking the purpose of the organization. This development which integrates freedom within a self-imposed discipline, results in the greater good of all, not self-interest at the expense of the common good (freedom without inherent order).

11. *The leader of the quantum system enables sub-systems to be optimized by working on the optimization of containing systems.* Hence, the individual good of each person is achieved as larger systems are improved for the common good.

Effective leadership is focused on finding the solutions for the future that reside collectively in the organization and enabling them to be implemented. This requires, at all levels, *living with substantial ambiguity and uncertainty and being comfortable with it.* Are you comfortable in uncertainty and ambiguity? What is your stance — intellectual, moral, social, spiritual, societal — in those circumstances? Can it be changed, developed, altered, enhanced? How do you see others in those circumstances? When you try to build a co-responsible team, a team that can take on change and challenge with a positive nature and a shared vision, you must examine your basic beliefs and leadership styles.

> In the post-bureaucratic world, the laurel will go to the leader who encourages healthy dissent, who values those followers brave enough to say *no*, who has, not the loudest voice, but the readiest ear, and whose genius may well lie not in personal achievements, but in unleashing other people's talent.
>
> Bennis, 1996: 15

Leaders need to be *able to recognize paradox* (fuzzy logic) — paradox in people, ideas, and feelings — and not be frightened of it. According to Lou Tice (1996: 19), during times of change there are two styles that are dominant: control and release. With the control orientation (finite world), you do not want ordinary human beings running around, messing up management's perfect world. With a release orientation (abundant world), you seek ways to work together. Rather than create restrictive zones, you create constructive zones at the 'edge of chaos'. Mother Teresa once said: 'I can do what you can't do, and you can do what I can't do; together we can do great things.' In times of change, unpredictability and uncertainty, one person cannot do it alone. You have got to create a critical mass around you of people who, in their own way, do whatever they need to do to build the community or organization toward a shared ideal. It takes a complementary team of people. Formally defined in the academic literature (for example Powell and Dent-Micallef, 1997), complementarity represents an enhancement of resource value, and arises when a resource produces greater returns in the presence of another resource than it does alone. It takes a team knowledgeable about each other's feelings, needs, hurts, pains, beliefs, and dreams — a real soulful community which is comfortable with, and understands, uncertainty and ambiguity. A team that is able to learn new things; quickly adapt in times of change and thrives on chaos. A team aware of the fact that whatever other changes may be required in its improvement efforts, the importance of these is greatly outweighed by the required changes of human minds — the minds of its members. Leaders of these teams need to understand that managing change is mainly a matter of managing psychological processes. Change becomes a positive adventure when people feel safe moving out of their environmental comfort zones, out of their narrow definitions (and mindsets) of the way things are supposed to be. Change begins with the realization that *one cannot manage people, one can only lead perspectives and perceptions of people*, thereby impacting on their goals, needs and passion. Therein lies the opportunity for growth and positive adventures.

In sum, leaders must observe whole systems while pragmatically setting boundaries around the aspects of the system they choose to address. However, while accepting limits, leaders need to remember that boundaries are artificial and permeable. Leaders must understand the relationships among the parts, the dynamics of the connections, and their interdependence, because it is in the *interaction* that the whole becomes greater than the sum of the parts.

> The spirit of a beehive, the behavior of an economy, the thinking of a supercomputer, and the life in me are distributed over a multitude of smaller units (which themselves may be distributed). When the sum of the parts can add up to more than the parts, then that extra being (that something from nothing) is distributed among the parts. Whenever we find something from nothing, we find it arising from a field of many interacting smaller pieces. All the mysteries we find most interesting — life, intelligence, evolution — are found in the soil of large distributed systems.

Kelly, 1994

Some leaders, such as Geoff Mordt, former managing director of Interpak Cape in South Africa, keep a journal to identify recurring problems not being solved with cause-and-effect thinking, and to identify systemic relationships within the distributed system (April, 1997). Solutions to such problems frequently lie in the dynamics of the relationships, in the patterns of the whole. Leaders must see themselves as farmers, not mechanics (Norgaard, 1996). Farmers do not ask:

'Which is most important, preparing the soil or selecting and growing the best seeds?' Likewise, leaders should not ask whether they ought to focus on changing the systems and structures or on developing the people. They must do both. When people change, our organizations change, and when our organizations change, people change. The new way of thinking — thinking on the 'edge of chaos', being comfortable with uncertainty, and thriving in ambiguity — stretches our minds, our abilities, our resilience, and our patience. According to Mette Norgaard (1996: 20): 'We may spend two years creating the conditions for collaboration, and where we see a fertile field others may see a pile of dirt. Still, as new growth emerges, the results speak for themselves'. Norgaard further asserts that, as we move from thinking 'I' to thinking 'we', from thinking of personal goals to thinking of team goals, our organizations, communities and families are transformed. As we combine our energy, creativity and commitment, we become resilient and adaptable during periods of drought, and unsurpassed during bountiful seasons.

Connectivity
Communication, Conversation and Dialogue

> These are complex issues, we must talk some more.
>
> *Native American tribal leader (from the film:* Dances with Wolves*)*

Diversity, collaboration and teams became increasingly important management and leadership issues during the 1990s — all of which are unattainable, both now and in the future, if we are unable to communicate, converse and have dialogue. As already seen, globally, and notably in South Africa, change is very much part of life as we embark on this new millennium. In the academic and popular literature, communication and conversation are often seen as tools for announcing and explaining change, preparing people for the positive and negative effects of change (Jick, 1993), increasing others' understanding of and commitment to the change (Beckard and Pritchard, 1992; Morgan, 1988), and reducing confusion about, and resistance to, change (Kotter and Schlesinger, 1987).

Kanter, Stein and Jick (1992) maintain that the key roles communication plays are providing and obtaining information, creating understanding, and building ownership. These perspectives treat communication as a tool that is used within a change process. We, however, like Ford and Ford (1995), and Zohar (1997), maintain that change is a phenomenon that occurs *within* communication, conversation and dialogue. This is in contrast to the notion that change is necessarily something that is forced on an organization from the outside. Even when change *is* forced from the outside (for example when a business is forced to confront new market conditions), we would argue that a dialogue process is critical for that change to be handled effectively.

Dialogue and metalanguage

'Dialogue' is the label given by British physicist David Bohm (1980) to a deeper level of communication which has a serious commitment to cooperation and behaviour congruent with the constructive thinking styles identified by Clay Lafferty in his *Life Styles Inventory*. The late Bohm, a theoretical physicist and author of many works about quantum physics, branched out, so typical of the new scientist, into many other disciplines and was particularly interested in the nature of thought and consciousness and how these get expressed in the way people communicated. He advocated the revival of an old Greek art form, the *dialogos*, as a means of bringing people together in communication that allows the surfacing of tacit assumptions and beliefs in a spirit of inquiry and respectful exploration. Another famous physicist, Werner Heisenberg (1958), once said, 'science is rooted in conversation'.

The word 'dialogue', as used by Bohm comes from two Greek roots: *dia* and *logos*, suggesting 'meaning flowing through'. This stands in stark contrast to the word 'debate', which means 'to beat down', or even 'discussion', which has the same root as 'percussion' and 'concussion', meaning 'to break things up'. Gerard and Teurfs (1997: 16) inform us that dialogue really consists of four skills and a set of guidelines. The four skills are:

1. *Suspending judgement*. Because our way of thinking divides things up and creates what seem like ultimate 'truths', it is difficult for us to stay open to alternative views. Our egos become identified with how we think things are — our reality. We defend our positions against those of others, and close ourselves off from learning and do harm to our personal relationships. When we 'suspend judgement', we see others' points of views; hold our positions lightly; and build a climate of trust and safety. As people learn that they will not be 'judged' wrong for having opinions, they feel free to express themselves fully. The atmosphere becomes more open and truthful.

2. *Identifying assumptions*. The opinions and judgements we hold are usually based upon layers of assumptions, inferences, and generalizations. When we ignore the underlying belief system behind our judgements, we make decisions that lead to disappointing results. Only when we peel away the assumptions can we see what might be giving us trouble: some incomplete or 'incoherent' thought. We can then explore differences, build common ground and consensus, and get to the bottom of misunderstandings.

3. *Listening*. The way we listen impacts how well we learn and how effective we are at building quality relationships. We focus on developing our capacity to stay present and open to the meaning arising at both the individual and collective levels. We can learn to listen and perceive at more subtle levels by overcoming typical blocks in our ability to listen attentively and to stay present.

4. *Inquiring and reflecting*. Through inquiry and reflection, we dig deeply into matters that concern us and create breakthroughs in our ability to solve problems. By learning how to ask questions that lead to new understanding, we accelerate our collective learning. We gain awareness of our thinking processes and the issues that separate and unite us. By learning how to work with silence, we can identify reactive patterns, generate new ideas, perceive common ground, and gain sensitivity to subtle meanings.

As people gather to dialogue, they commit to a common set of guidelines:

- Listening and speaking without judgement.
- Acknowledgement of each speaker.
- Respect for differences.

- Role and status suspension.
- Balancing inquiry and advocacy.
- Avoidance of cross-talk.
- A focus on learning.
- Seeking the next level of understanding.
- Releasing the need for specific outcomes.
- Speaking when 'moved'.

Bohm (in Jaworski, 1996: 110) points out that a great deal of what we call discussion is not deeply serious, in the sense that there are all sorts of things which are non-negotiable — the 'undiscussables'. No one mentions the 'undiscussables' — they are just there, lying beneath the surface, blocking deep, honest, heart-to-heart communication. Furthermore, we all bring basic assumptions with us — our own mental models, or what Colin Hall calls 'mental pictures' — about how the world operates, our own self-interests, etc. Our basic assumptions are developed from our early childhood days, our life experiences and socialization, our peers and family, our education and reading. We hold these assumptions so deeply that we become identified with them, and will defend them with great emotion and energy when they are challenged. Quite often, we do this unconsciously. Jaworski (1996: 111) makes the point that, 'If there was an opportunity for sustained dialogue over a period of time, we would have coherent movement of thought, not only at the conscious level we all recognize, but even at the tacit level, the unspoken level which cannot be described.

Dialogue is a difficult and uncomfortable concept as it is about insight as the source of action. Dialogue requires that leaders reveal their logic and hold up and reveal their assumptions and beliefs, rather than their arguments, for scrutiny. It is interesting that so many ancient cultures seemed to engage in the practice of sitting in a circle and talking and talking until, as many Native American Indians say, 'the talk starts'. Maybe this is the fit of the new sciences to the ancient cultures of the world, to say, 'you were right after all!' We think that the old cultures had a clearer understanding of new science — the old cultures of Africa, the old cultures of the Aztec, the Inca cultures, the native American cultures, the aboriginal Australian cultures. It is clear that many such cultures do not hold the view that is so common in the West today, that thought is a purely individual phenomenon, occurring within our own heads. Apparently, one reason the Greeks considered *dia-logos* so important was their view that it was vital to self-governance. Once a society loses this capacity, all that is left is discussion — voices battling it out to see who wins and who loses. There is no capacity to go deeper, to find a deeper meaning that transcends individual views and self-interest.

Gerard and Teurfs (1997) write that through dialogue and conversation, community is created and culture transformed in three ways:

- *Behavioural transformation.* Participants learn how to be with each other differently. They practise skills and guidelines that encourage new norms. The more these are practised, the more dialogical communication is used — leading to the actual state of community.

- *Experiential transformation.* Dialogue and conversation sets up the conditions of community. While groups new to dialogue will not be in full community when they first start out, the atmosphere induced by dialogue and conversation has the 'experiential feel' of community. Individuals thus learn what a culture based on community principles *feels* like, and they incorporate it at an intuitive level.

- *Attitudinal transformation.* As group members experience the effects of dialogue, a profound shift takes place at the belief and attitude level. Attitudes of rigid individualism give way to attitudes of collaboration and partnerships. Beliefs strengthen around the 'value of the group as a whole'. As groups progress in their ability to use dialogue, they move to higher levels of problem-solving and problem-finding.

The reason that we see dialogue as critical to any change process, is that when we examine how leaders make people aware of key concerns or shifts in organizational focus, it is readily apparent that their questioning style has a pervasive effect on how organizational members direct their attention. Used effectively, questions can concentrate the mind and set the agenda. We sometimes have to question how these questions are used — whether this leads to leaders imposing their personal agendas on others. Colin Hall, in addressing the 1998 MBA Leadership Class at the Graduate School of Business (UCT), made it clear that in a previous leadership role (and previous mindset for him) as a director at multinational brewing giant, South African Breweries, he was able to focus people's energies, time and effort in a direction which he saw fit at the time. He admits that this was not always congruent to what the employees wanted, felt or desired. In contrast, Arnold Mindell (1992) in his book *The Leader as Martial Artist*, recommends somewhat different principles for a leader to follow, namely that leaders work with the natural energy of their followers that arises from changing moods, tensions, emotions, roles, and time spirits. The narrow path that the leader must follow is a path that the followers themselves create and can accept, and to realize that the energy of their followers cannot be completely controlled or predicted.

According to Stephen Covey (1997), the deepest part of human nature is that which urges people, each one of us, to rise above our present circumstances and to transcend our nature. If you can appeal to it, you tap into a whole new source of human motivation. In 1970, Robert Greenleaf made the point that the forces of good and evil, in the world, are propelled by the thoughts, attitudes, and actions of individual beings. Greenleaf, along with John Gardner and James MacGregor Burns describes how leadership is more than skills and situational know-how: it is, instead, and more fundamentally, a moral contract between leaders and followers to bring out the best in each other for the good of the whole. Leaders should pay attention to the informal channels by which organizational messages are conveyed.

When countries or organizations make major changes, they often proclaim new symbols and discard or destroy old symbols and artefacts in favour of the new. We need look no further than the toppling of the Berlin Wall, and certain statues in South Africa, for dramatic evidence of this. Leaders are attentive to the use of ceremonies, both official and spontaneous, in the reinforcement of shared values. Rory Wilson, ex-managing director of Independent Newspapers (Cape) (now CEO of Juta), went as far as having a ceremony of the slaughtering of a goat and wearing skin bracelets during the shaky period of credibility and trust formation in the take-over of the black newspaper, *The Sowetan*, by a traditionally white media company, the Argus Group. What does this communicate to the people, both in the organization and its customers? Many ask, 'Was it necessary to go so far?' However, in the South African context, is this not the type of intentional change, and courage, we are looking for?

According to Kouzes and Posner (1995: 229): 'In the performing art of leadership, symbols and artefacts are a leader's props. They're necessary tools for making the message memorable and sustainable over time.' The sensitive and intelligent management of those 'tools and artefacts' can be vital in how particular sectors of a leader's followership will respond to future challenges and ideas of the leader. This was seen in the South African Parliament, when certain paintings and pictures were removed from the halls. However, they were not discarded. Instead, Mandela, who was President of South Africa at the time, insisted that they should be put in prominent positions in museums and galleries, since 'they are part of our history and culture'. This action has had far-reaching effects for Mandela's credibility as a leader, especially among the white Afrikaner sector of the population.

We believe that when an individual has *less concern for the ego associations of leadership, and more for the mission to serve by liberating and redirecting individual resources and energy, potential expands*. People do more than they had been doing because they feel freer to be more than they had previously felt it possible to be. As a result of the greater energy available, through the more actualized individuals, there is more possibility for creative change in organizations. This requires those in the organization to think and act beyond their functional domains, and to work in an alignment similar to that required of players in a symphony orchestra. With a high degree of interdependence required to optimize such a system, serious attention is paid to open communication and conversation, dialogue, collaboration, and the innovation required to achieve the aim of the system. A special effort is required to equip leaders to lead this kind of organization and community.

Intentional change

Poole and DeSanctis (1990) observe that change as an organizational phenomenon necessarily occurs in a context of human social interactions, which constitute and are constituted by communication. These interactions produce and reproduce the social structures and actions people know as reality (Berger and Luckmann, 1966). From this perspective, change is a recursive process of social construction in which new realities are created (Ford and Backoff, 1988), sustained and modified in the process of communication and conversation. Producing intentional change, then, is a matter of deliberately creating, through communication, conversation and dialogue, a new reality or set of social structures. If this is the case, then the change process actually occurs within, and is driven by, communication, conversation and dialogue, rather than the reverse. It is our assertion that intentional change is produced through the development of these conversations and dialogue. Ford and Ford provide us with the following definitions:

> Intentional change occurs when a change agent deliberately and consciously sets out to establish conditions and circumstances that are different from what they are now and then accomplishes that through some set or series of actions and interventions, either singularly or in collaboration with other people. The change is produced with intent, and the change agent is at cause in the matter of making the change. Unintentional change, in contrast, is not deliberate or consciously produced, but is manifested as side effects, accidents, secondary effects, or unanticipated consequences of action.

Ford and Ford 1995: 543

We therefore propose the following guidelines (April, 1999: 236–239) to provide a plan for organizations to start thinking about how to produce change in the psychological structure of individuals within the organization — to move as many as possible of their organizational members toward exercising transformational leadership — by employing notions from systems thinking methods, scenario planning, and organizational learning. What is important to remember when dealing with the psychological structure of individuals is the personalities of those involved in the change process; the history of the individual and the organization; and the manner in which the change is introduced (Willcocks and Rees, 1995). It points to the value of open and honest communication when attempting to avoid defensive behaviours that are grounded in misinformation.

Creating space for dialogue and conversation

We believe that it will become important in twenty-first-century organizations to create 'special places' that are more conducive to dialogue and conversation than traditional conference rooms. Dixon (1998: 103–104), stresses the fact that these are 'less formal spaces, often with comfortable couches and overstuffed chairs. They have more natural lighting than the harsh fluorescent lights of conference rooms and they typically have coffee and refreshments handy . . . The walls of the room are covered with whiteboards, filled with diagrams, lists, pictures, quotes, charts and other thinking tools teams have used.' Studies have shown that the availability of community common rooms actually serves to increase team member collaboration (Wild, Bishop and Sullivan, 1996). A number of forward-thinking organizations are leading the way in thinking about space for dialogue by designing special 'dialogue common rooms' where informal conversation and personal interaction can occur, for example Hitachi, America Ltd., National City Bank, and Owens Corning. Old Mutual in Cape Town, the largest insurance firm in South Africa, and SAS Airlines in Stockholm, for example, have 'central plazas' in the midst of their corporate headquarters, which contain shops, cafés, hair-dressers, travel agents, and so on, where people from all levels and functions are encouraged to visit and share ideas. Dixon (1998: 104) stresses the point that 'these designs reflect the increasingly relational nature of our work and the impor-tance of creating space that accommodates a more relational kind of talk'.

Generating organizational awareness — 'communities of practice'

It is important that the leadership of the company be, and is seen to be, involved in the change process. Part of that responsibility is to develop a methodology that will systematically help individuals get past the stumbling blocks that have pre-vented dialogue and conversation before. Coupled to that is the need for dialogue settings — 'communities of practice' — in which people can reflect about their accomplishments, their frustrations, their attitudes, and tell their personal stories in their own words. At the Graduate School of Business of the University of Cape Town, we encourage students to go beyond the obvious, to venture beneath the surface, and teach them that through true conversation and dialogue, they are able to build deep trust and respect for one another. It is in settings such as this that we get an idea of how wonderfully enriching and informative, how powerful our theories and related practical applications can be if we only allow *all kinds of minds and people* to be equal in our lives (Evans, 1999). In this way, through the medium of communication, we intend to help each student get beyond the deval-uing prejudices that we all hold, so that true teamwork can be built among groups. Trust is considered here to be emotionally based, but with a cognitive component, and dependent on the belief in the reliability of oneself or the other person or group. It can only be given by each person, not demanded. Without this type of dialogue as input, individuals within the organization will not develop a rich enough level of content, not just about the event, but about the systemic structures and mental models that exist below the surface.

Argyris and Schön (1978) have correctly argued that organizational perform-ance problems are more likely due to a lack of awareness and inability to articulate and check underlying assumptions, than to poor efficiency. This points to the importance of understanding how individuals perceive, interpret and respond to changes (both internal and external) in the organizational 'communities of prac-tice'. In particular they must be aware that, as a result of personality and experi-ence differences, reality is subjective, and this needs to be understood both by leaders and by followers. The idea behind generating awareness is therefore to bring out the unexpected relationships and fundamental causes that have been hidden underneath the noticeable and significant symptoms that everyone sees.

Feedback

Feedback is very important to the individual change process, and can occur on two levels: from within a group and/or individually. For feedback to be effective, organizational mentors (trained organizational psychologists, or trained management coaches) are important — they provide the important link between people's experiences and organizational life, for example through note-taking during conversation and dialogue sessions, mentors capture and help construct stories, and gather data from a wide enough group of people so that judgements can be made about whether or not a story is typical. This means listening to what people have to say, asking critical questions and engaging people in their own inquiries. Mentors also continually make sure that the evolving research methodology of the process is rigorous.

Group feedback

Developing trust between individuals involves encouraging all the members of a group to reveal thoughts and feelings about themselves to others through self-disclosure, and by getting feedback from others. By being able to accept risk, an individual can become more creative and open to the possibility of being able to develop sustained intimate relationships. And, in a country such as South Africa, where racial groups have forcibly been kept from communicating, perhaps we can all move closer, through conversation and dialogue within a context of trust, to experiencing what deep alignment in a group or team feels like — the resurrection of a country's buried energy, soul and life force.

In the workplace thi's has particular relevance. If people are willing to communicate openly different kinds of information, including their fears and feelings, the result will be that they will be more willing to inform change rather than resist it. This has direct relevance to what Giddens (1994: 119–121) refers to as the 'democracy of emotions', which means that individuals will not only be in contact with their own feelings but will be able to openly express these to others in a democratic manner. This requires a reflexivity of oneself, and being able to reflect on actions and values. Individuals are encouraged to raise issues about any barriers (perceived or real) that might hinder individual or team effectiveness. In this sense, trust goes beyond basic rational cooperation and becomes an emotional force that can be called upon in risky situations to allow us to go on. But if cooperation increases when conditions are unpredictable, because people realize that their futures depend on each other, then, where organizations face turbulent change, trust-building is vital. Managers should regard dialogical communities of practice as company assets and look for ways to preserve them (Davenport and Prusak, 1998). On the other hand, where organizations see people only in terms of being resources, then only adaptive learning can be achieved (versus generative learning), since individuals will not be able to express themselves fully, nor identify with their work community and organization in the long term.

Developing trust between individuals involves encouraging everyone in a group to reveal thoughts and feelings about themselves to others through self-disclosure, and by getting feedback from others. By being able to accept risk, an individual can become more creative and open to the possibility of being able to develop sustained intimate relationships. As more and more individuals within the organization become involved in and committed to the change process, the system becomes more and more effective. Along with involved leadership, there needs to be more than one 'champion' who sets the stage for individual change and learning. This is particularly necessary in learning that is related to changing a basic value or a long-cherished method. The greater the number of advocates who promote a change culture, the more rapidly and extensively the learning will take place. This paves the way for the development of a culture that will build awareness of the team concept and support critical individual change initiatives.

Individual feedback and reflection

The judgements people make about themselves, and others, are not always concrete or obvious. They can be abstract and highly inferential, but sometimes individuals treat them as if they were concrete because they produce them so automatically. It is therefore important to have individual feedback sessions within organizations, where skilled organizational psychologists, or management coaches (personal mentors), can assist individuals during their sense-making and change initiatives. This mentoring process has to be designed so that judgements, inferences and interpretations can always be linked to actual data (sourced during dialogue sessions). The ideas of clinical research interviews (Schein, 1987) and creating reflective settings should guide this process. Individuals can be assessed (formally or informally) to determine how well their skills and abilities match the identified, required behaviours within the reflective spirit that prevails in the organization.

People are encouraged to identify personal competencies required for effective performance and change in a future-oriented organization. It is also the platform from which mentors can get a sense of the individual's readiness for change. In addition, reflective interviews give participants a chance to talk openly and expressively about their experience — a significant source of learning in itself. Mentors need to deliver comprehensive feedback that compares performance against critical competencies — this then leads into the development of personal scenarios (see below) for individuals. They also need to ensure that participants receive accurate and reliable information about their progress through a carefully designed individual-performance management system. It is during these individual sessions of dialogue that individual anxiety concerning change, and individual defence mechanisms, can be explored. Several authors have examined the idea that formal and informal aspects of organizations act as defence systems against anxiety (Willcocks and Rees, 1995; Menzies Lyth, 1988; De Board, 1978). De Board (1978) argues that defence against anxiety is one of the primary aspects bonding individuals together in organizations, making for cohesion. Anxiety in organizations, as in individuals, is a symptom of fear or the perception of danger. The existence of anxiety, and the defence against anxiety are important, therefore, in understanding organizational effectiveness and change.

Conversational bank

A 'conversational bank', or discussion database, is a repository in which participants record their own experiences on issues (organizational, personal, political, and so on) and react to others' comments. This is an electronic repository (operated through an Intranet or similar network), similar to Davenport and Prusak's (1998) 'knowledge repositories'. Through a combination of face-to-face interaction and electronic communication, vital relationships within the organization can be established and maintained. The growing popularity of teamwork makes the notion of a 'conversational bank' increasingly important as a success factor on an organizational level. The 'conversational bank' should be judged by the quality of the conversations it provokes.

Keeping a diary — self-reflection

Reflection is widely recognized as a crucial transformational element in the learning process of individuals (Schön, 1983; Mezirow, 1990; Rigano and Edwards, 1998). Efforts by some major companies, such as PepsiCo, Motorola and General Motors, to harness reflection as a deliberate tool for learning is a significant trend towards addressing the need for formal reflective practices in the workplace (Daudelin, 1996).

The process of reflection is important for the integration of new experiences with past experience. Critical self-reflection has much in common with the action learning approach of Revans (1978; 1982). Butler's (1994) model of human action and change indicates that professional growth comes from continuing cycles of action and reflection. Reflection is the process which 'can modify personal knowledge, beliefs and actions' (1994: 21). The use of journal writing has emerged as a significant introspective tool for promoting individual reflection for personal professional growth. For example, Marsick (1990) outlined ways for facilitating reflection in the workplace and identified journal writing as a useful tool for helping people become aware of their own practical reasoning and theory building, and to make explicit their tacit knowing. Daudelin (1996) developed the 'reflection workbook' which provided guidelines for the use of a learning journal to record and explore the random thoughts and summary learning statements that occur throughout a work experience. Barclay (1996) provided practical guidelines for the use of 'learning logs' for recording and enhancing experiential learning. She identified some key features of self-development embodied in the learning log: personal development planning (which ties in with the personal scenarios discussed below), learning responsibility, and individuality of the method.

From the mentor perspective, clear purposes and expectations, and access to skilled mentor support, are required for inexperienced journal writers to avoid superficial and non-reflective entries, and to overcome the uncertainties and frustrations associated with acquiring new skills. Many business schools, such as the Graduate School of Business at the University of Cape Town, now make use of journal writing as part of their leadership development programmes for MBA students. It is important that lessons learned from journal writing be used in the development of personal scenarios, in order to encourage ownership of the reflective process by the participant — vital for maintaining the necessary motivation, discipline and interest.

Personal scenarios

A scenario is a tool for ordering one's perceptions about alternative future environments in which today's decisions might play out. In practice, scenarios resemble sets of stories, written or spoken, built around carefully constructed plots. Stories are an old way of organizing knowledge and experience, and when used as planning tools, they defy denial by encouraging — in fact, requiring — the willing suspension of disbelief. Stories can express multiple perspectives on complex events, and scenarios give meaning to these events. Personal scenario planning will enable individuals to imagine, and prepare for, discontinuous change through systematic and recognizable phases. What increasingly affects all of us, whether professional planners or individuals preparing for a better future, is not the tangibles in life — bottom-line numbers, for instance — but the intangibles: our hopes and fears, our needs, our beliefs and dreams. By moving from being tacit to explicit through dialogue and conversation, only stories and our ability to visualize different kinds of futures (personal scenarios) adequately capture these intangibles.

Individuals are therefore encouraged to design and implement a carefully planned, high-involvement, individual change strategy, that is, a personal scenario(s), around five thrusts:

- communication,
- skills,
- accountability,
- collaboration, and
- systems (process improvement).

These strategies, borne from their personal scenarios, teach them to envision multiple futures for themselves, their team members and the organization. These must be clear and can be very specific. For example, an individual can develop a personal strategy by identifying a vision (the 'where'), the values (the 'how'), and critical success factors (the 'what') to bring about the desired change. If individuals, with the assistance of mentors, are prepared to look at the world in non-traditional ways; challenge their assumptions about the future; and test the viability of their personal strategies in various futures, scenario-based personal planning is the best way to accomplish this.

Implications for leaders

So what does intentional, or unintentional, change mean for leaders? Quite simply, that they open themselves in communication, conversation and dialogue, to input from those they lead. This, often, can be a frightening experience and requires great courage from leaders. Moreover, it is our belief that everything, including leading the pursuit of change, begins with the initiative of the individual. It may be argued then, that part of the responsibility of leaders should also be to allow people (others) the space, time and energy to expose their true feelings, beliefs and attitudes — both to themselves and others. This requires creating opportunities for individuals to meet others in intense engagements, through conversation and dialogue, which hopefully changes and shapes the way they experience each other. In facilitating and encouraging communication, conversation and dialogue, the leader allows a whole spectrum of possibilities to open up. In this way, individuals are able to develop their own capacities to go deeper, to find deeper meaning that goes beyond self-interest and individual viewpoints. The challenge of creating such opportunities for self-expression is that people are often not equipped to speak about their personal feelings. Certainly, in the experience of the authors, a significant amount of re-learning needs to take place — whereby people learn a vocabulary of 'feeling words' — to enable a platform for open communication to be ultimately productive. In addition, a culture of patience needs to be developed, so that those who are not speaking, listen, and ensure that the speakers are acknowledged and heard. A lack of patience on the part of listeners can undermine the sincerest of efforts to facililate open communication, conversation and dialogue.

Presently, in organizations, families and communities, people operate separately, often creating barriers between each other by their fragmented thought — thought resulting from age-old thinking, no longer relevant in our chaotic world. According to Peter Senge in *A New View of Institutional Leadership*:

> Once a society loses this capacity [to dialog and converse], all that is left is a cacophony of voices battling it out to see who wins and who loses. It seems reasonable to ask whether many of our deeper problems in governing ourselves today, the so-called 'gridlock' and loss of mutual respect and caring . . . might not stem from this lost capacity to talk with one another, to think together as part of a larger community.

Adapting to change takes time, because it is not just a rational process, but will always involve a degree of emotional acceptance on the part of those affected. Where change is disruptive, emotional commitment will be needed to cope with the loss. Change will be perceived as interfering with our sense of adaptation by appearing to overwhelm our structures of thought which make sense of the world (Marris, 1974: 15–18). Managing change is directly related to the level of trust engendered in the individual and in groups. Where trust is high, change is managed more effectively, and, where it is low, communication and cooperation will suffer and there will be an increasing tendency to resort to power. It is our firm belief that part of the healing of South Africa's soul lies in the art forms of conversation and dialogue, sometimes referred to as 'surface-to-depth conversations'.

The work of the Truth and Reconciliation Commission (TRC) may be seen in this context, attempting to contribute to healing the nation's soul through open communication, conversation and dialogue. The challenge, in South Africa, is for courageous organizational leaders to take definite steps forward, based on trust and respect, toward creating forums, time and space for all the people within their organizations to openly communicate, reflect, converse and have dialogue — to talk about their families and their personal crises, and to express their hurt, pain, joy, beliefs, feelings, anger, future goals and dreams, and to discover one another's 'undiscussables'.

Until people are able to do that in their organizations, employers must continue to expect employees to bring 5–10 % of themselves, and their energy, to work . . . and the vision and mission of the organization's executives will stay just that — the vision and mission of the executives, rather than 'being felt and lived' by willing, enthusiastic and energized followers within the organization. It should also be clear that, as more control is used by leaders, employees will have less trust in the process (Handy, 1985: 327).

That communication and conversation play an important role in the production of change is not an entirely new concept. One can go back as far as Socrates, two-and-a-half thousand years ago, to his use of conversation as a method for seeking deeper understanding . . . a way of seeking the rock-bottom truth in what was being discussed. He taught Western civilization the art of asking questions as a tool for discovering reality. For Socrates, 'the unexamined life was not worth living'. In modern organizations, the depth conversation in the Socratic mode is coming into its own again. This is fostered through the creation of continuous learning opportunities; promotion of inquiry and dialogue; encouragement of collaboration and team learning; empowerment of people towards a collective vision; and the establishment of systems to capture and share learning (Watkins and Marsick, 1993). As more and more leaders shift toward participation and empowerment, they are beginning to learn the Socratic way of processing information through asking the right questions, instead of making pronouncements and giving orders. What we constantly hear is that, the more people practice the art of orchestrating conversations and dialogue, the more opportunities they find for it: processing office flare-ups; reviewing and reflecting on the day, month or year for evaluations, for making group decisions, even for office celebrations. In dialogue, the goal is to create a special environment in which a different kind of relationship among parts comes into play — one that reveals both high energy and high intelligence (Jaworski, 1996). In a learning organization, dialogue provides ways for teams and groups to reflect constantly on their experience and learn from it.

Conversation and dialogue forces one, in a sense, to make explicit the things we could not previously talk about, the things that hindered true and real friendships. It is our experience that, *once you are real, you cannot be non-real again*. The challenge for leaders is to find and meet the energy and, hence, the meaning in people's lives, by constantly digging and naming what they find in their communication and dialogue with others. As we know, not everybody will like and be happy with what has been dug up, but leaders need to foster experiences that allow individuals to coalesce around issues of shared concern and move forward to successful resolution of those issues. We therefore propose that leaders, hoping to be successful in an ever-changing and chaotic world, need to create opportunities in which others can find, for themselves, balance, meaning and fulfilment. Essentially, this can only be achieved through the leaders and their followers being in an ongoing state of connectedness. Technology has allowed connectivity to become a buzzword for the twenty-first century. In keeping with its meaning, connectivity too, will be a key aspect of leadership in the new millennium.

Process
Strategy and Leadership

Instead of looking for particular leverage points, a living systems thinker might listen for where the system wants to go. By amplifying or intensifying people's overall awareness of that direction, new behaviours will naturally emerge, and propel the overall pattern of the system across a threshold into a new form.

Roberts and Kleiner in The Dance of Change

'No aspect of corporate life is indifferent to strategy. Every problem leads to strategic solutions' (Zaleznik, 1992: 130). The challenge of developing or re-establishing a clear strategy is often primarily an organizational one, and often depends, rightly or wrongly, on leadership. 'With so many forces at work against making choices and trade-offs in organizations, a clear intellectual framework to guide strategy is a necessary counterweight. Moreover, strong leaders willing to make choices are essential' (Porter, 1996: 77). Strategic planning is considered to be a major part of the leadership function of an organization. Colin Hall says that 'an organization is really a strategy . . . it's a strategy to achieve an objective, a vision, a series of visions, or a whole series of possibilities' (April, 1997). When strategic planning arrived on the scene in the mid-1960s, corporate leaders embraced it as 'the one best way' to devise and implement strategies that would enhance competitiveness and growth. True to the scientific management, pioneered by Frederick Taylor, this 'one best way' involved separating thinking from doing.

Traditional organization theory mandates that we design organizations and try to plan outcomes, thereby conditioning us to assume that there is no alternative. However, traditional strategic planning appears to be facing an identity crisis of major proportion. In particular, Mintzberg (1994) has developed an exhaustive case for why strategic planning, as classically conceived, cannot succeed. The essence of his argument is that planning, as a decompositional, analytic activity, is processually and structurally incompatible with effective strategy formulation, an act that largely requires creative synthesis. According to Mintzberg's reasoning, planning should be kept conceptually and operationally distinct from strategy formulation. He argues that decisions in organizations are usually taken on a trial-and-error basis, with only partial understanding of the situation. Many strategies, 'post-hoc rationalizations of activity', emerge gradually over time, that is, incrementally. Cohen, March and Olsen (1972) say that decisions are often not 'taken', but 'happen'.

They suggest that moments of decision occur when four independent streams happen to coincide: 'problems', 'solutions', 'participants', and 'choice opportunities'. Problems demand attention; solutions are answers looking for problems; participants are the constantly varying crowd of organizational actors carrying different problems and solutions; and choice opportunities are occasions when organizations are expected to make decisions. According to Cohen and his colleagues, organizations are like 'garbage cans' into which these four independent elements are thrown together and shaken until a more or less random conjunction produces a decision — the outcome of near chance collisions between problems and solutions.

In understanding organizational strategy, Mintzberg and Waters (1990) provocatively suggest that decisions 'get in the way'. Rory Wilson alluded similarly when he claimed that, if he had a wish list, it would be to stall meetings from making decisions — since the real creativity and energy of his organization is in the coming together of its people and the ensuing processes that take place (April, 1997). In organizations, we conventionally assume that decisions represent commitments to future actions. However, decisions in practice are often followed by no actions, or even by quite different actions from those we intended. Conversely, actions are not necessarily the outcome of any identifiable single moment in action, that many traditional leaders would like to believe. New science theory tells us that events often take on their own momentum, with decisions only flickering on the surface. A great deal of our behaviour is not 'decided' at all. The best leaders may be the ones who take the fewest conscious choices.

Even 'emergent' or 'incrementalist' strategies offer little guidance to leaders struggling with the problem of navigating their companies in the present, and future, uncertain world. Most of these theories are based on linear logic, where cause and effect are closely linked. Ralph Stacey (1995), however, argues that neither approach is adequate for our purposes. Fortunately, insights from studies of complex natural and organizational phenomena enable us to address the problem of strategy and uncertainty. Stacey, Beerel and Pascale have written extensively on the management of chaos, and its conjugate, complexity. Research has revealed that systems tend not to gravitate toward chaotic behaviour, but rather toward an area of complexity between chaos and order. Managers and leaders operate in an unpredictable world, and the environment cannot be effectively controlled, because even quite minor changes in apparently isolated phenomena can provoke major changes in the total system. So, for example, the flapping of a butterfly's wings in Brazil may make a difference between calm weather and a tornado in Texas (Gleick, 1987). Stacey (1995) believes that organizations must accelerate their creative ability and generate new strategic directions faster than their rivals. He suggests that leaders are constrained by their existing mental models into travelling well-worn paths of success. We agree with Stacey when he claims that 'these paths can be both easily emulated and lead to stagnation'. The nature and magnitude of dynamic environmental change requires leaders and managers to defy their natural tendency towards business-as-usual. Success lies in the area of creating new paths, new capabilities and competencies, and not in the imitation and refining of old ones. Studying successful organizations and blindly adopting their approaches does not provide sufficient tools for coping with future challenges. Organizations must *create a mindset of change*, a new paradigm, that is not only receptive to, but also guides transformational change. Pascale (1993: 291) offers four key ideas that underlie the quest for this new organizational reality:

1. Organizations must accept the premise that their current management and leadership mindset is self-limiting.
2. Organizational attributes and behaviours that lead to stagnation, and those that encourage renewal, should be identified.
3. Conflict, as an ever-present force in organizations, must be harnessed constructively.
4. A new definition of leadership and management roles must be sought to reconcile the tensions inherent in an organization living on the edge of its own paradigm.

Leadership and planning have always been about analysis — about breaking down a goal or set of intentions into steps, formalizing those steps so that they can be implemented almost automatically, and articulating the anticipated consequences or results of each step. 'I favour a set of analytical techniques to assist leaders in developing strategy', Michael Porter, probably the most widely read writer on strategy, wrote in the *Economist* in May 1987. This analytical, linear notion of leadership and leaders' ability to plan for the future is based on three assumptions:

1. that long-term prediction is possible;
2. that leaders can be detached from the subjects of their strategies, plans and choices; and
3. that the strategy-making process of leaders can be formalized.

In 1965 Igor Ansoff wrote: 'We shall refer to the period for which the firm is able to construct forecasts with an accuracy of say, plus or minus 20 % as the planning horizon of the firm.' According to Langley (1991), it does not matter all that much if planning from leaders in an organization comes out with the 'wrong' answers, as long as the planning process is allowed to fulfil control, social and symbolic functions that otherwise the organization might fail to achieve. 'In an institutional environment valuing quantification and rationality, the planning process, however expensive in time and effort, may be a necessary sacrifice to cultural expectations' (Langley, 1991: 132). For Hax and Majluf (1995), planning techniques employed by leaders introduce a qualitative element complementary to the quantitative bias of necessary financial calculations of net present value.

Mariann Jelinek (1979: 139) developed the interesting point that strategic planning by leaders is to the executive suite what Taylor's work-study methods were to the factory floor — a way to circumvent human idiosyncrasies in order to systematize behaviour. According to her, if the system does the thinking, then strategies must be detached from operations, formulation from implementation, thinkers from doers and leaders from the objects of their strategies and choices. The trick, of course, is to get the right information to leaders — hard data, quantitative aggregates of the detailed 'facts' about the organization and its context, neatly packaged and regularly delivered. With such information, senior executives and leaders need never leave their executive suites and staff offices.

We propose a new way of looking at leadership and its role in organizational behaviour by introducing several relationship-based questions.

- How do we get people to work well together?
- How do we honour and benefit from diversity?
- How do we get teams to work together quickly and efficiently?
- How do we resolve conflicts?
- How do we grow people so that they can add value for their company, their community, their society, and their country?
- Is strategy relevant?
- Are concepts like 'organizational vision' and 'mission' still valid?
- How do we partner with our suppliers, previous competitors and suppliers, to create more energy, more possibilities?
- What are the enablers of synergy in embarking on strategic partnering?

The role of business in both creating new world realities and formulating a response to those realities is now centre stage. The realm of business decisions, according to Beerel (1998: 27), can no longer confine itself purely to factors that influence the economic bottom line. Social, cultural, religious, demographic and political issues need to be understood as the critical, relational inputs and outputs of business processes. The new leadership, for example, excels in strategic partnering and recognizes that all participants in the system are potential partners. The construct of adversary, Beerel informs us, is no longer apposite. Those who held opposing views and engaged in competitive activities are now viewed as complements, rather than antagonists.

Strategy viewed from this perspective takes courage, commitment to the common purpose and an ability to be true to the organizational values and principles, irrespective of costs and personal risks. However, like Evans (1999), we believe that the new, necessary leadership will only arise in organizations where democracy is allowed to flourish. Currently, true democracy in organizations is a rarity. Perhaps this is why the new forms of organization are emerging with unprecedented speed — evidenced by the shake-up of traditional workplaces, and the phenomenal growth of Internet- and Web-based companies. One such example is the new, exciting m-commerce project undertaken recently by the Sanlam Digital Commerce Group (Sanlam is South Africa's second largest insurance firm). Sanlam was known, within the business community of South Africa, as a company which was traditional in its approaches, staid in its ideas and a good example of the 'old mindset'. However, it has now found ways to free up energy — through strategic partnering and developing a 'servant-leadership' culture — which otherwise would have been used for 'beating' or 'outmanoeuvering' the opposition. So much so, that its Digital Commerce Group is not even concerned about the competition — in their own words: 'We are not trying to find a place for ourselves in the industry, we are, instead, creating a new industry!' Strategic partners and energized Sanlam employees are engaged in a new and completely different strategic and negotiating mindset. Driven by CEO, Hannes van Rensburg, the Sanlam Digital Commerce Group made sure that, from the outset, they established the ground rules for the culture they were trying to create, the ground rules for developing and empowering people, the ground rules for establishing, maintaining and growing relationships, and the ground rules for keeping each other excited and passionate in the workplace — in this way, being able to continuously self organize in response to the energy and information that flows to their organization from the environment.

True leadership, in our opinion, is dependent upon *respect for the complex network of people who contribute to the organization*. The actual configuration of relationships within a business organization determines how an organization actually executes its strategy, and does its business. In his book, *Leadership is an Art*, Max De Pree's (1989: 11) advice for leadership was deeply consonant with the systemic and interrelatedness concepts of the new science. According to him, leaders should liberate people to do what is most required of them: to change, grow and strive for their potential. Any meaningful strategic process must be able to encapsulate such liberation. Organizations can only do this if they are aligned to the changing realities of the world and are in touch with the consequences.

> The organizations that get things done are no longer hierarchical pyramids with most of the real control at the top. They are systems — interlaced webs of tension in which control is loose, power diffused, and centres of decision plural. . . . Because organizations are 'flatter', more horizontal, the way they are governed has to be more collegial, consensual, and consultative. The bigger the problems to be tackled, the more real leadership is diffused and the larger the number of people who can exercise it — if they work at it. The trend is as visible in totalitarian as well as democratic societies. 'Collective leadership' and committee work are not conclusive evidence of democratic feeling. They are imperatives of bigness and complexity.

Cleveland, 1997

Organizations' structures continually need to change in order to facilitate and enhance their ability to execute strategy and deliver a distinctive product or service. This creates the opportunity for people to exercise their diversity of skills, talents and understanding of a particular situation — different people should be given the freedom, space, resources, and encouragement to exercise their leadership skills.

The new South African leadership understands that there are multiple, equally valid realities held by diverse groups from different cultures and diverse walks of life. These realities are understood to be part of the fabric of a diverse, vibrant and creative world — a world with infinite opportunities for everyone. Wheatley (1992; 1999) believes that the current movement toward participation and collaboration in the workplace through the use of teams and quality principles, is rooted in the new sciences and chaos theory. The new focus on relationships within leadership follows science. In fact, the new adaptive leadership in the organization is attuned to the multitude of new realities that are continuously being unveiled, and they need to ensure that the organization, threatened by changing values and the pace of change, does not take flight into preoccupation with technical fixes (Beerel, 1998).

Colin Hall makes the point that 'strategy is not something that you can stop and set. It's using the resources you've got in the most experiential and organic way to arrive at better outcomes' (April, 1997). Effectively, what Hall is saying, and what we assert in line with new science thinking, is that strategy is about process, and that the leader needs to develop a keen understanding of process. By 'process' we are referring to the 'experiential and organic way' about which Colin Hall speaks. It is about understanding relationships, group dynamics, creating rich connections, how to catalyse ideas from others, being happy with ambiguity, and not rushing for certainty. In other words the skill is to focus, not on the outcome of the strategic development process, but rather on the process itself. This understanding is critical for leaders who will be operating in the new world where the focus is no longer on things, but on processes.

Followership
A Personal Reflection on Leading by Following

Roger E. Breisch

[The] critical breakthrough occurred when self-awareness connected to his conscience as he worked on his [personal] mission statement. It became emotionally cathartic and prepared him to receive feedback from other people. This feedback enabled him to see things in a true light, which compounded his awareness of the incongruencies between deeply held values and his work style. Because he exercised his moral agency to choose in that moment, his awareness both deepened and expanded, and his power and freedom to choose his response to other circumstances increased.

Covey, 1999

Our Western culture is, I believe, overly focused on control, answers, personal prestige, material possessions, winning and success as defined by ascendance to the highest heights. Humble, soulful qualities are often considered less desirable. It is a culture in which the dominant model of leadership is highly influenced by a Newtonian world-view. Newton, who first proposed the laws of motion, believed that the cause-and-effect relationships of physical motion could be accurately described. The future, if you will, of balls on a billiard table could be foretold if sufficient information was given regarding the initial conditions. At the macro level, Newton was right. For hundreds of years, knowing nothing of quantum mechanics, we were happy to assume that these Newtonian laws of cause and effect applied throughout the universe. It led us to live our lives with the mistaken belief that, given sufficient information about initial conditions, the future of the world could be accurately predicted.

We were also led to believe that feelings, actions and thoughts will act in much the same simplistic, predictable way. We were raised with a deep belief that the world could be 'figured out'. Given enough brain power — or computer power — we could take our knowledge of current conditions; implement specific actions or interventions; and ordain a knowable, predictable future. Further, we use this predictive capability not only to know the future, but also to know the precise steps needed to get from here to there. What makes this insidious, is that most people will say, verbally, that we cannot predict the future, but will act as if the results of their actions are knowable. The most hurtful indication of this for me is the way I all too often treat my children as if I knew what was best for their future!

When Newtonian views are used, defining leadership becomes an easy task. We look for a person with the following three things: the best description of current reality, a clear picture of the future we wish to share, and a precise list of steps to get us from here to there. We see the effects of this thinking everyday. One of the most common complaints we hear of senior managers is that they have no vision. If they have a vision, the most common complaint is 'they're not good at day-to-day management', which usually means they cannot tell us the appropriate steps to get us there. Our clients want us to accurately describe their current pain; paint a vision of how tomorrow can be better; and show that we have the precise intervention to get them from 'pain to gain'.

Not only is this an unrealistic description of leadership — I do not believe it describes the kind of leader to whom we are actually drawn. I believe that revered leaders such as Mahatma Ghandi, Nelson Mandela and Martin Luther King Jr. did not know precisely what the future would look like or the precise path they would follow, nor did they understand the repercussions of the actions they took. While each had a broad vision, it was probably not a precise and accurate picture of how the future would look or evolve. Their leadership emerged based on something broader than a cause-and-effect view of the world. Newtonian physics is not wrong, it is simply far too narrow in its ability to explain human behaviour.

Around the globe, we see the Newtonian bedrock being questioned. Now we must question whether some theories about organizations, management and leadership are still too narrow in their ability to explain what actually emerges in communities of people.

The problems with the cause-and-effect model of leadership

Before I discuss what leadership might be, I would like to return to the old model and describe what I see as the inherent flaws; why leaders seldom understand current reality, have a clear view of the future or know how to get us from here to there.

A leader should have the best description of our current reality

I have often displayed the Kanizsa triangle (Figure 7.1) to large groups and asked whether the white triangle is larger or smaller than the black. While it is seldom unanimous, the majority typically agrees they are, in fact, the same size. I then ask how many in the group *believe that there are <u>no</u> triangles in the picture*. It contains six independent shapes arranged so they look like small pieces of two triangles. This usually yields a combination of laughter, confusion and debate about how the group was 'tricked'.

Rather than a cute game, I see this as a powerful metaphor for the kind of thinking we do all too often. We, speaking personally, take incomplete bits of information about the world and use them to construct larger, complete pictures

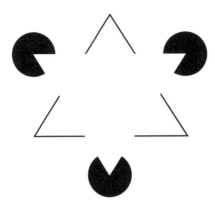

Figure 7.1
Kanizsa triangle

— mental models we then use to 'understand' how the world works. How many times have we, as parents, done this with our children? We walk into the house after a long, stressful day and see thirty seconds of activity and turn it into a complete picture of what they are up to, including, who did what to get them upset, their motivation, what they were thinking and why they are wrong! We are fully prepared to create a vision of the future, along with action plans based on an incorrect description of the current reality. Usually, when we take a few moments to inquire into the situation, we find we have constructed their current reality in inappropriate ways. While I would like to believe otherwise, we know we have made this same mistake with co-workers and friends.

Chris Argyris (1990; 1993) created a wonderful tool, the ladder of inference, to describe this way of thinking. Imagine a ladder with five rungs between the bottom and top. Each rung represents a step in the process we use to turn sensory data into action. The first represents unfiltered data — the nearly infinite amount of sensory information we are subject to at any moment. Rung two represents the way in which we filter it. None of us is able to deal effectively with all of it, so we select that which captures our attention, and we each do it differently. Ask a group of people to close their eyes and list what they remember about the room they are in. You will get as many different lists as there are people. Next — rung number three — we are busy adding meaning to the data we have selected. To me, a piece of paper on the floor may mean the conference centre staff does not pay attention to details. To you it speaks of the attitudes of the participants. After we add meaning, we make assumptions — rung four. Based on everything we believe about how the world works — our mental models — we build an ever-larger picture of what the data means. 'If the conference centre staff is willing to let paper lie on the floor, they are obviously lazy or poorly trained.' On the final rung, we act. 'I would never schedule a conference at a place like this.' While this is a simplified example, many of us climb this ladder in about three nanoseconds, hundreds of times each day! Fortunately or unfortunately, this is a reiterative process. Each time up the ladder, we use the results of previous iterations to add to our personal views of how the world operates.

To say that a leader should have an accurate description of current reality is a misnomer; no one has! To make matters worse, many managers take their inaccurate definition of current reality a step further. They are so busy tending to the administration of their business that they refuse to take time to see their employees' and customers' current reality at first hand; they rely on the inaccurate descriptions of others. Tom Peters created an entire management style — management by walking around (MBWA) — precisely because managers were too far removed from day-to-day events to have any accurate picture of current reality.

For a number of years, I worked for a Fortune 500 company. One of the major divisions of the company was sold as a leveraged buy-out to the management. The CEO of the newly created company commented that in the 15 years he ran it as a division, his boss, the CEO of the Fortune 500 company, *never once left the executive wing and visited the division headquarters, let alone other facilities in the division!*

Shortly after the book *In Search Of Excellence* (Peters and Waterman, 1982) was published, this same CEO 'declared' there would be a new culture. As part of this new culture, senior executives began a series of 'informal' communications lunches — scheduled six months in advance, held in the CEO's private dining room and catered by the executive chef. My turn came about a year later. The executive vice-president invited me to one of these 'informal' lunches. There were five attendees in addition to the vice-president: the vice-president of R and D, the president and vice-president of the division where I worked, and two middle managers, including me, who were encouraged to speak honestly. The executive vice-president started the lunch by asking the two of us what we thought of the new culture (current reality). I told him I thought nothing in particular had changed. His reaction was interesting. He told me I was wrong. The reason he knew was because after many of these lunches, I was the first to express that belief. About six months later an employee attitude survey confirmed what I had told him. No one had noticed. Everyone in the informal communications lunches told Frank what he wanted to hear, that everything was going great. Frank was a very smart individual who had been with the company his entire career. He *knew* the culture did not allow *him* to speak freely to senior managers when he was in the trenches, yet he believed that everyone was being honest with him.

Many of us fall into that trap. When we are middle managers we tell our bosses how wonderful they are and we are embarrassed when they believe us. Yet, when we get there and people tell us how wonderful we are as managers, we congratulate them for being honest. 'Yes,' we tell ourselves, 'we really are much better than those managers before us who were simply gullible.'

What does this imply about leadership? 'Good leaders articulate what people really need, but only when they understand what the need is. Then the power comes from the people, not because the leader tells them what to do, but because the leader is describing what they want and filling a void' (Barciela, 1998: 105). As reality is socially constructed, the 'best realities' — believable, and able to get the buy-in of willing followers — are those that are constructed together, in a shared manner, inclusive of all affected by it, and through it. 'As individuals telling our stories to one another, we create an interpretation of our lives, their purpose and significance. And through shared stories, we see patterns emerge that unite our separating experiences into shared meanings' (Wheatley, 1998: 340).

A leader has a clear picture of the future we wish to share

We often refer to this as vision. Leaders are expected to have one; those without vision are criticized. We talk eloquently about the power of vision. 'If you don't know where you are going, any direction will do', is the admonition often heard. Unfortunately, we confuse vision as a compelling sense of direction, with vision as a precise picture of what the future should look like. 'Life is,' as John Lennon said, 'what happens when we are making other plans.'

In a recent interview, the pianist Michael Jones was asked about the importance of vision — having the end in mind? Michael said:

> There is a wonderful interplay between mastery and mystery. On one hand, you have the mastery of having and fulfilling a vision. But along with vision is imagination. Imagination is the path the heart loves to wander. You find yourself in places you had not conceived. The things I encounter at the piano I had not anticipated are the moments of grace I live for. If it was only hearing something in my head, then getting it on the piano, I don't think that would be enough to keep bringing me back. It's the mystery of finding things happening in my hands . . . composing through my fingers. This is not so much vision as it is life of the imagination . . . Unfortunately, we've been taught that the future we ordain can be fulfilled the way we ordain it. If we live according to those rules the possibilities open to us become limited . . . it becomes a relatively narrow life.

Warren Bennis, in his classic book, *On Becoming a Leader* (1994b), says: 'The first step toward change is to refuse to be deployed by others and to choose to deploy yourself.' 'Vision' defined as someone else's precise picture of the future, leaves little room for 'life of the imagination'. It is the interplay of mystery and mastery that leaves us inspired and motivated. We need vision as direction, with room to deploy our own imagination.

There is an additional aspect of vision on which I wish to comment. We want, and need, people to be motivated and inspired by their lives and their work. Not too long ago I came to the realization that the word 'inspired' and the word 'spiritual' have the same root. The words 'motivation' and 'emotion' also have similar origins. I, like many people in the workplace, find it difficult to be inspired and motivated unless there is a spiritual and emotional content to my work. Money and status are not enough to satisfy people at work. Most people, I believe, want to feel that they are engaged in something bigger than they are. It is so easy to become someone you do not want to be, even without realizing what is happening. To the extent that a leader can paint a vision that has a deep emotional and spiritual context, people will be more fully engaged in the enterprise. If the vision is only inspirational to the leader who is bringing it forth, it will have minimal effect.

A leader has a precise list of steps to get us from the current reality to the future we desire

It is said that every action we take has intended and unintended consequences . . . the intended consequences sometimes happen, the unintended ones always do!

During the US administration of President Dwight Eisenhower, the United States built a highway system that connected all the major cities in the country. While there were a number of reasons to justify the investment, one line of reasoning was that the highways would save the declining inner cities. The logic was that by facilitating the movement of goods and services into the cities they would become more available and cheaper. What actually happened? People fled. The highways made departure from the inner cities so easy that suburban areas grew almost overnight. It was suddenly possible to live outside the older areas of the city, show up from eight to five for employment, and retreat to a new home in a nice neighbourhood for dinner. This 'saviour' of the cities actually may have hastened their decline!

Not too many years ago, it became clear that washing clothes in a wash basin took too much time and effort. An automatic washer would save people a great deal of time. Do people spend a great deal less time doing laundry today? While it may have been reduced a bit, the unintended consequence is that we have dramatically increased the variety of clothes we wear. Few people would consider wearing the same clothes for more than a single day without cleaning them — teenagers seldom go more than a few hours! Along the way, we have revolutionized the fashion industry. Since we cannot wear the same clothes, or even similar ones, two days in a row we need to have a wardrobe that shows we have a wide selection from which to choose.

Tax authorities argue that commercial development is beneficial because it will increase the tax base. Commercial development, we are told, will help keep our property taxes low. A recent study of numerous American cities shows that, over time, commercial development and property taxes go up together — lock step.

Peter Senge (1990a) said that the solutions we implement today will often lead us to even bigger problems tomorrow. Gary Hamel (1996: 74) made the point that '. . . the terrain is changing so fast that experience is becoming irrelevant, even dangerous'.

There is an experiment which is sometimes referred to as superstitious learning. You take a cage full of birds and throw them food at random intervals — no rhyme or reason for the timing. Unfortunately, they do not know the food is arriving randomly. They conclude that their behaviour has brought about the feast. 'Wow! If I flap my wings and food appears. I'll try it again.' And away he goes. Another begins to hop feverishly. A third begins to chirp. Soon the entire cage is filled with elegant dances and wonderful singing, each bird absolutely convinced that its particular behaviour is causing the food to arrive. Imagine, if you will, some new bird introduced into the cage. Everyone he talks to gives him his personal cure to end 'world' hunger. 'Just flap like this.' 'No no no, that's not the answer . . . hop on one foot.' 'Bull, if you want food, you have to chirp . . . three short chirps followed immediately by one long, high-pitched whistle.'

What happens next? One of them decides, 'Hey, there will be other new pigeons arriving soon and they'll give me some of their food if I show them how to get more.' The advent of the feathered consultant. Richard Farson (1996) points out the futility of this thinking: 'If you find a management technique that works,' he says, 'give it up!'

Stephen Covey (1996: 3) claims that leaders have to start living more out of their imagination than their memory. He makes the point that Arnold Toynbee's observation, 'nothing fails like success', is very relevant today. Yesterday's success is just not equal to the new challenge, and so both leaders and followers must constantly develop new character sets, mindsets, and skill sets. Finding the way to authentic awakening presents us with an immense challenge.

Leading by following

So where does this lead? The likelihood that any of us will dramatically improve our businesses — or our lives — by following someone else's successful strategies and tactics is slim. The more we incorporate other people's silver bullets into our organizations, the more we begin to dance like pigeons.

Warren Bennis (1994) simply says: 'Becoming a leader is synonymous with becoming yourself'. 'Healing the universe', Fiitjof Capra (1996) once commented, 'is an inside job'. It was ee cummings who said, 'To be no-one but yourself in a world which is doing its best to make you just like everybody else, means to fight the greatest battle there is or ever will be' (Firmage, 1994). These are powerful thoughts. They say that leadership comes from deep within, and not from external views or visions. Effective leaders put words to the formless longings and deeply felt needs of others. 'They create communities out of words. They tell stories that capture minds and win hearts' (Bennis, 1996). Through conversation and dialogue we discover who cares about what, and who will take accountability for next steps.

Leadership, I believe, emerges from *clarity of self*. The more that individuals know what is truly important to them — and what the values are to which they are deeply committed — the more clearly they will see the path that they need to walk, and step out in boldness toward that path. The leadership we seek lies within each of us.

Michael Jones, the pianist, spoke about finding his path. Michael did not sell his first CD until he was 38, but has since sold over 1½ million copies. In spite of falling in love with the piano at age two, he was unable to admit to himself and others that his gift lies in his music. He set out to become a management consult-ant and change the world through ideas; ideas carefully constructed by others and repeated by him. Michael found his gift partly because an elderly gentleman in a quiet hotel in Toronto, happened upon Michael playing a piano, thinking he was quite alone and 'safe'. This wise man, touched by the wonderful sensitivity of Michael's music, looked at him and asked, 'Who will play your music if you don't play it yourself?' Michael said, in commenting on that chance meeting, 'I didn't know what to say. I just sat there stunned!'

In Illinois, there is a learning laboratory for the very best high school-aged maths and science students in the state. It is known as the Illinois Math and Science Academy (IMSA). Stephanie Pace Marshall is the current President and one of three founders. Before co-founding IMSA, Stephanie was superintendent of schools for Batavia, home of the Fermi National Accelerator Laboratory. She had a promising and predictable career in school administration. One fateful day, she heard Leon Lederman, then director of the Fermi Lab, give an impassioned talk on the urgent need for a place of learning dedicated to maths and science. Stephanie, feeling a deep calling to this work, called him the next day and set about the task of creating a new environment for learning. Together they convinced the Governor and the State Legislature to fund this unique and untested idea.

A Chicago artist, Andrew Young, is beginning to make a reputation for himself on the world stage. Andrew had a promising career as a scientist, with many opportunities to pursue research and academia. 'In college I had a very strong love for art but didn't feel it was appropriate to pursue it full time; in fact, I was very much afraid of it. I had a lower drawer at my desk, sort of my "altar", filled with pastels, watercolors, watercolor pads and colored pencils, all of which were impec-cably arranged, neatly sharpened and color-coded. Three semesters in succession I signed up for and withdrew from a course in color and composition because I knew what kind of door it would open. At the risk of sounding arrogant, I suppose I knew I had something; I knew I had a great deal of passion for the subject. I was almost like a closet art lover: reading magazines when I should be looking at some-thing else, going to art museums when I said I was going to a sporting event. I was trying to conceal something that was clearly boiling in my spirit. As far as the soul and the things that I recognized could be explored and expressed in art, the power of that relationship was overwhelming.'

Recently Tim Gallwey, author and tennis star, spoke of the way in which we normally teach sports. He likened it to a rubber mat with footprints. Unless the student steps on the footprints in precisely the correct way, they are doing it 'wrong'. What he came to learn is that the body has an innate sense of movement. The secret to improved athletic ability is to get the mind out of the way — thinking impairs natural ability. Now we should be asking ourselves, what would it look like if we stopped trying to live our lives as if we had to place our feet on the correct space on life's 'rubber mat'. What would it mean if we followed our deep desires?

What would it mean to get thinking out of the way — out of the box — and make room to live life more naturally? For me this means living the life of the heart.

Michael Jones (1995) made the point that 'our way of experiencing life, and our participation in it, becomes the art of all arts', and discussed the poet, William Stafford:

> Stafford wrote a poem every day . . . a tremendous output for a poet. Robert Bly once asked how he was able to accomplish that. He said, 'First, I lower my standards!' Then he said a wonderful thing. He got up in the morning, sat, and waited for the first impulse. He would treat that impulse as the golden string, and follow it into the poem. As long as he was obedient to that authority, the thread would lead him into the poem. The important thing was not to pull on the string because he would break the connection.

In recent years, I have had the privilege to know many people who have created wonderful institutions, art, music and ideas. All of them are living lives largely dictated by beliefs, values and passions which, they would say, are often beyond their control. All can point to significant moments when they needed to make choices, and they *chose to follow their passions*. So, there is the conundrum. They lead precisely because, at the critical moment in their lives when they were called, they followed. The individuals described above followed that inner voice that called to them. Listening inwardly, they came to understand what they needed to let go of and what they needed to develop. They took incredible risks. Yet, they chose the difficult, but extraordinarily joyful path — the path their heart called them to. Based on logic, analysis and cultural norms, each of them could have chosen a path of less risk — a path of greater predictable security and of less joy. But each of them chose a path of courage. Each of them leads by following.

Stewardship
The Leader as Servant

But there are also people in organizations who come from a place of contribution. They look at the world through the lens of abundance. They are willing to give to others first while not worrying about what they are getting in return. Because of their positive outlook, sense of appreciation, and trust in others, they attract more things to appreciate and trust in their relationships. These folks are like gardeners, cultivating their relationships and nurturing them with trust.

Reina and Reina, 1999

Traditional, autocratic and hierarchical principles of leadership are slowly yielding to an alternative concept. This concept attempts simultaneously to enhance personal growth of workers and improve the quality and caring of our many institutions. This is achieved through a combination of teamwork and community, personal involvement in decision making, and ethical and caring behaviour. This emerging approach to leadership and service has been termed 'servant-leadership' (Spears, 1995). The term 'servant-leadership' was coined and institutionalized in 1983 by the late Robert K. Greenleaf, director of management research at AT&T and founder of the Centre for Applied Ethics. Larry Spears, the current executive director of the Centre for Applied Ethics, says that the concept involves 'increasing service to others, taking a more holistic approach to work, promoting a sense of community within an organization and between an organization and the greater community, sharing of power and decision making, and a group-oriented approach to work in contrast to the hierarchical model' (1995: 196).

'Servant-leadership' is an interesting term, a juxtaposition of apparent opposites, an oxymoron that immediately causes us to think afresh. This phrase leads us into a different universe, one which is more congruent and meaningful for us in our present-day world. It's a universe where our sense of self is very different, a universe toward which all the esoteric and spiritual traditions point, and a universe which, we believe, most of us are hungry to participate in. Our personal understanding is that servant-leaders see their primary responsibility as one of *service to those within their sphere of influence*.

By drawing on the work of Gibson (1998), we propose a six-theme framework from which to better our understanding of this fascinating, and relevant, concept.

Servanthood

The word 'servant' has negative connotations for some people, especially those who have previously been oppressed in South Africa. However, if one thinks of a servant as a 'nurturer of the human spirit', 'inspirer', it conveys a much more positive tone. According to *Webster's New World Dictionary*, the word 'inspire' means 'to breathe life into'. It also means 'to cause, communicate or motivate as by divine influence'. It is a powerful word that paints a picture of someone or something beyond ourselves, infusing us with a purpose or a mission, and calling us to action. The modern world has stifled much of the creativity of its leaders, by concentrating on a rational and analytical approach to leadership. This has tended to suppress the spontaneous, intuitive and inspired nature of our current leaders. The idea of the leader as a servant first (as popularized by Greenleaf), provides a sense of release by giving us *permission to serve and inspire others* — harkening to our calling. It also introduces a spiritual element into leadership and stresses the importance of compassion. John Gardiner muses about how the world would be different if the principle of assisting or serving others was viewed equally with that of gaining for one's own (in Spears, 1998) — then service above self could lead to the changes that would bring about true global renewal.

Leadership as a state of being

Jaworski (1996) speaks of 'predictable miracles' that occur in our lives: how doors open when we are ready to walk through them, how we encounter people or ideas at exactly the right moment. Jaworski makes the point that leadership is much more concerned with 'being' than 'doing'. It is about our orientation of character, our state of inner activity. He was greatly influenced by the writings of Greenleaf, who asserted in *The Leader as Servant* that there are two dimensions to leadership. The first is the *desire to serve others*. The second is the *desire to serve something beyond ourselves* — a higher or overarching purpose. 'I have often wondered where this "feeling that one wants to serve" comes from — my conclusion is that it comes to us as a calling and often manifests itself in our work' (Jeffries, 1998: 30). In fact, the word 'vocation' — otherwise known as our work, our personal work (not only meaning our jobs) — comes from the Latin word *voca*, which means 'to call'. We believe that everyone has a vocation, and that we all are called to a unique purpose — the place where each individual's maximum energy resides. According to Michael Novak, in his book *Business as a Calling: Work and the Examined Life* (1996), a calling has four characteristics:

1. Each calling is unique to each individual. A calling causes a desire and, often, a passion for doing something that you simply can't say no to.

2. A calling requires certain preconditions. One is talent. You may love opera, athletics or business, but a desire in itself does not make it a calling. Another

precondition is love — not just of the final product, but as essayist Logan Pearsall Smith said, 'love of the drudgery it involves'.

3. A true calling reveals its presence by the enjoyment and sense of renewed energies its practice yields us. We are willing to shoulder the burdens of the calling because we know it is part of what we are meant to be doing.

4. Callings are not usually easy to discover. Many false paths may be taken before the fulfilling path in uncovered.

Greenleaf viewed our purpose as something to strive for, to move toward, or become. Most of us avoid taking the journey to discover and serve our purpose — our higher calling. We tend to deny our destiny because of insecurity, self-doubt and the fear of risking what we have. One of the main reasons we refuse the call is because we know deep down that, to cooperate with fate not only brings great personal power but also *great personal responsibility* — and often, not the power, social, financial and material rewards that the Newtonian business world can offer us. It takes much *courage to cross the threshold* — the edge — that marks the start of this journey. However, when we follow our purpose, a sense of flow develops and we find ourselves in a coherent field of others who share our sense of purpose (Jaworski, 1998).

Business leaders discover the purpose or destiny of their organizations in the same way that they discover their own purpose or calling. Writers such as Hamel and Prahalad have indirectly alluded to this — discovering and nurturing the core competencies of an organization; those competencies that maximize the energy, abilities, and talent of the specific organization. Organizations too, are embarking on a search to discover their 'calling' — for most of the time, muddling through, just like we do in our lives. 'When the searches of an organization and its leaders run parallel and then converge, a great explosion of energy and creativity takes place' (Jaworski, 1998: 263). Those who would be servant-leaders must come to grips with who they are and where they are on their journey. On this journey, the direction — the process — is more important than the goal or destination, which will be revealed in due course — but we must *learn to trust the journey (trust the process), trust ourselves and trust others*. That thought is captured in the words of the Spanish poet, Machado, who states: 'Wanderer, there is no path. You lay a path in walking' (Jaworski, 1996: 134).

Stewardship

Stewardship is different from ownership. Stewardship implies a trust in the sense that you represent someone or something else. Ownership is usually about 'me' and 'mine'. Ownership is a clear expression of independence; stewardship is a clear expression of interdependence, which is the nature of the new work contract — the new psychological agreement. We are interdependent, and we cannot just go our own way. To achieve a state of stewardship, one of the prerequisites is that you *first give something up before you get something back*. We may give up not only material things, but also the pride and arrogance of 'me' and 'mine' in exchange for a humble heart and a contrite spirit, for an ethic of service and sacrifice (Covey, 1997: 3).

Citizenship and community

One of the pillars of servant-leadership is the concept of community. It seems reasonable to ask whether many of our deeper problems in governing ourselves today might not stem from the lost capacity to talk to one another, to think together as part of a larger community (Spears, 1995: 228). Interestingly, the contemporary metaphor of 'organizational development' is gradually giving way in our organizations to an older metaphor, 'community building'. A community comprises people and how they interrelate. As we begin to understand that the current organizational metaphor is becoming increasingly inappropriate, we continue to pursue basic questions like: 'How do shared visions develop?' and 'How can widely shared mental models change?' Can an organization 'have a vision', or 'hold a shared mental model', or 'learn'? Mike Levett, chairman of Old Mutual, expresses a similar concern when he states that 'organizations don't feel' and 'organizations don't learn — people feel and learn' (April, 1997). Ken Blanchard, co-author of *The One-Minute Manager* series, informs us that, in his research and talking to corporate presidents, a common notion (such as Levett's) among the traditional leaders is held. Surely this is a classic case of reification, of treating an abstraction as if it actually existed. So perhaps we have been misleading ourselves for many years when we have spoken of 'building a shared vision for an organization'.

We, however, believe that *communities can hold visions, can feel and share assumptions, and enhance collective capabilities*, that is, learn. As thinking about shared vision, shared mental models and group learning changes, from something which cascades down through an organization from the top, to something which emerges amongst a group of people as they engage in dialogue and conversation, the metaphor of communities becomes more appropriate. A community can have a shared vision, shared assumptions and can learn, since it is made up of people in meaningful relationships.

Peter Block (1998: 90) urges a shift in our focus from 'leadership' to 'citizenship'. He writes that to keep focusing on the selection, training and definition of leaders is to stay frozen in the world of monarch, autocrat and entitlement. It postpones the day when people will experience a world of community and accountability. The question of citizenship stays in the background, in the shadow of the attraction to leadership. If citizens instead ask their leaders to sit down with them, to join them; learning then replaces instruction, participation replaces presentation, and questions become more important than answers. Block defines citizenship as an agreement to receive rights and privileges from the community and, in so doing, to pay for them through a willingness to live within certain boundaries and act in the interest of the whole.

At the core of citizenship is the desire to care for the well-being of the larger institution. Are you acting in the interest of the whole in your particular context — be it your family, your workplace, your church, your neighbourhood, your society, your country? This requires *accountability*. Each person can be a role model, walking the talk, articulating longings, offering hope and inspiration. This is the nature of citizenship. When these tasks are left to leaders, people are let off the hook and conspire to create a culture of entitlement instead of a culture of accountability. Clinging to the attraction of heroic leadership keeps change in the hands of the few — the future requires that it is transferred to the hands of many. This is the power of citizenship. From the new sciences we learn that nature and particle physics teaches us a new form of democracy — a democracy more akin with servant-leadership and citizenship. The bias towards monarchy, and belief in the centrality of the leader, makes people ignore collective and communal successes and celebrate the heroism of the individual. If society can learn to let leadership be, and choose to focus on citizenship, the knowledge and experience exist to create accountable institutions. This is an important step towards an accountable culture, which is the essence of democracy (Block, 1998).

The servant-leader

Although the terms 'servant' and 'leader' are generally thought of as opposites, when these opposites are brought together in a creative and meaningful way, a paradox emerges. This paradoxical idea of servant-leadership is offering hope and guidance for a new era in human development. The real leaders in any group of people are not necessarily those who are the formal persons in charge of the group. Often emergent informal leaders, on whom the group comes to depend, prove to be of much greater importance. *Servant-leadership requires humility of character and core competency around a new skill set* — not just directing, motivating and evaluating people using traditional performance appraisals. Perhaps there is no room for the word 'leader' in a system of management fundamentally predicated on inter-relationship. Garth Eagle, training manager of Caltex South Africa, says: 'I think we're in the era of what I would call the servant-leader . . . where the leader is quite clear on where he or she wants to go and then be the support person, to assist people to get there' (April, 1997). What matters is whether a shared vision exists, which is quite different from people following someone else's vision. New visions can emerge from many different sources, not just from 'the top'. Greenleaf talked about the 'first impulse' of servant-leaders — always to listen first, and not to talk. A proper sense of servanthood will result if leaders keep in mind that they have been chosen by those whom they serve and are answerable to them (Erickson, 1985).

The task of leaders is to make sure that good ideas are brought into the open, are considered seriously and, where possible, tested, so that eventually shared visions develop. Perhaps the essence of human experience is to discover connection to everyone and everything. In that case, the leader's role is to help others discover the paradox that they must take their own journey and that they are not alone (McCollum, 1995). True leadership emerges from those whose primary goal is a desire to help others — it begins with the natural feeling that one wants to serve. Then conscious choice brings one to aspire to lead. The difference manifests itself in, what Senge (1990a) terms, 'creative tension'. The best test, according to Green-leaf, is: 'Do those served grow as persons? Do they, while being served, become healthier, wiser, freer, more autonomous, more likely themselves to become serv-ants?' (Spears, 1995: 4). Ken Blanchard states that his aim in talking about serv-ant-leadership has always been to encourage managers to move away from the traditional direct, control, and supervisory approach to the roles of cheerleader, encourager, listener, and facilitator.

Helping to create the future

The future is not something 'out there', but rather *something we create at every moment*. 'By our efforts we bring the future into the present' (Greenleaf, 1983). Jaworski (1998) believes that individuals participate in creating their future, not by trying to impose their will on it, but by deepening the collective understanding of what wants to emerge in the world, and then having the *courage to do what is required*. By listening to signals — 'faint signals', as White, Hodgson, and Craner (1996) term it — people gain that sense of how the future is unfolding that enables them to cooperate with their, and others', calling. Servant-leaders have the respon-sibility to discover and serve their own destinies, as well as those of people around them and their organizations. 'Thus a world of predictable miracles and synchro-nous events opens to us, a world in which we can create the future into which we are living' (Jaworski, 1998: 267).

It is our opinion that South African organizations concentrate far too much on the technical, so-called hard skills, side of things rather than on the cultural and people side of things, because it is a whole lot easier to manage and deal with. The myth has to be dispelled that the so-called 'soft issues' — issues relating to people, leadership, and organizational behaviour — are easier to do, manage, and compre-hend. In fact, we would venture to say that it is precisely those things that are the hardest for people to be successful at, hence the tendency to avoid them. We would like to challenge all our readers to walk the talk of servant-leadership. Stephen Covey (1994: 3) provides us with some guiding principles — three initial steps to start us on the journey.

Build a new relationship

The new relationship is horizontal, not vertical, and is based on the principle of mutual respect and equality — not on power and position within the organization. The leader views the roles of worker, manager, and leader in a new light. The roles are equal, but different. Only when the leader has built relationships of trust does he or she have the foundation necessary to set up a meaningful performance or psychological agreement.

Create a new psychological agreement

The agreement represents a clear, up-front mutual understanding and commitment regarding expectations in five areas:

1. Purpose — specify the quantity and quality of desired results.
2. Guidelines — focus on principles, not on procedures, policies or practices.
3. Resources — identify available human, financial and physical resources.
4. Accountability — schedule progress reports and specify performance criteria.
5. Consequences — state both positive and negative rewards that reflect the natural consequences of actions taken.

The new agreement gives the other person total freedom, within the guidelines, to accomplish objectives. The moment such an agreement is set, the leadership paradigm shifts from one of benevolent authoritarianism to one of servant-leadership. The leader becomes a source of help to those individuals who have entered into this agreement. The accountability process is based on self-evaluation, using feedback from different stakeholders. Stephen Covey often refers to this agreement as 'stewardship delegation', since in such agreements each person becomes a 'steward' over certain resources and responsibilities.

Rory Wilson (now CEO of Juta) describes his approach when he was managing director of Independent Newspapers (Cape):

> The way I've been dealing with the complexity of the problem is . . . I've got fourteen people on my executive, inclusive of myself. I've said to the other thirteen, 'You run your business your way'. So the Editor runs his business — I don't interfere with him. I'm here to support him. The analogy is rather like the conductor and the orchestra, the conductor can be a superb conductor who may not even play the piano, or the violin, or the drums, but conducts the orchestra. And what we've now come to realize is that you have to let every person do their own thing, because there are not enough hours in a day and, because it works better that way.
>
> *April, 1997*

Transfer power and responsibility for results

Once the new performance agreements have been established, with clear understanding of common purposes and a deep buy-in by all parties, then people can do whatever is necessary within the guidelines to achieve desired results. The leader then takes the position of a servant and facilitator. She or he is no longer the one who directs, controls, or judges. Instead, she or he becomes a coach and resource who can interpret the data or lend experience, but the individual or team makes most decisions — including staffing, budgeting, and coordinating. If the person or team hits a brick wall, or finds the resources and guidelines insufficient, the leader may have to revisit and renegotiate the performance agreement with them. Covey (1994: 3) suggests that, in the mutual accountability sessions conducted by the person or the team, the servant-leader should ask four questions:

1. How's it going, or what's happening?
2. What are you learning from this situation?
3. What are your goals now?
4. How can I help you?

These questions keep the person responsible and accountable for results. Without that new mindset and skill set, servant-leadership will not work.

We support Peter Block's (1993) concept of stewardship. Cutting-edge scientific exploration is generating new support for the concept of servant-leadership. This research reveals that the most successful organizations (plant and biological) found in nature, are self-organizing, and relationships are a key building block, an integral part, of nature. Servant-leadership appears to be an appropriate philosophy for their governance. Wheatley (1992; 1999) says what you need is common vision, common purpose, and free information flow, because 'it's going to be chaotic, and you've got to expect it. But use chaos to your advantage. Let people have whatever information comes in, and then become a source of help to them.' The servant-leader principle requires a *change in attitude* more than a structural change. The servant-leader often has to *help expand vision and perspective*, and then bring to bear his or her experience — but, people want it! According to Covey (1994: 4), 'They're asking for it, because their lives are at stake. They know that their organizations are fighting for their economic life. And so the people, working under the servant-leader, have more responsibility and accountability. They're at the controls and sense that they're in charge, that this isn't a game anymore, that there's something at stake here.' To operate in this mode, leaders have to shed their egos and deeply embrace the belief that people perform best in an atmosphere of freedom and trust. Servant-leaders, according to Melrose (1996: 20), serve people not to get more out of them, but because they want to boost people's self-worth and dignity.

Greenleaf (in Spears, 1995) proposed that, if leaders could answer the following four questions in the affirmative, they were on the right path:

1. As a result of your leadership, are those whom you serve growing as persons?
2. Are they, while being served, becoming healthier?
3. Are they becoming more autonomous, freer, wiser, more capable?
4. Are they, themselves, more likely to become servant-leaders?

In addition to simply saying 'yes' to these questions, it is important to understand *how* we need to think to arrive at those answers. *What* we think, inevitably flows from *how* we think.

As we start this new century, we find contemporary scientific thought and long-standing spiritual thought converging. In that convergence, servant-leadership takes on more profound importance, since leadership is about the relationship of an organization to its environment, as well as about the way in which elements of the organization relate to each other. Essentially, what the new scientists are saying, is that stewardship is a great, and necessary, starting point — but it is a transitional stage.

The ultimate destination for leaders is the realization that people and teams are quite capable of being self-managed, that organizations require something very different from the current definition of leadership, and that organizations do not require nearly as many leaders as we would like to believe. Garth Eagle (in April, 1997) makes the following point: ' . . . what I believe to be important is the fact that leadership in an organization doesn't have to only be at the top. Leadership in an organization can be at any level.' 'But we, as followers, have to give up our search for the perfect leader and give up the urge to turn it over to someone who will not take care of it, but at least gives us a reason for criticizing them. We need to give that all up' (Wheatley in London, 1997: 4). On the other hand, we believe that leaders need to ultimately give up even the belief that it is their task to set the vision of the organization. They have to give up their belief, that if they do not design the organization, it will not structure itself.

Ambiguity
Leadership Incongruities, Tensions and Paradoxes

Susan Hill

The seeds of the future
Lie in the present

Adair, 1990

The theory and reflections introduced throughout this book contain, inherently, a certain degree of paradox and incongruity. Many explanations may be sought for paradox, incongruity and tensions within literature on leadership and how leadership is played out in reality. Possible explanations may include:

- a reflection of transitions in paradigms on organizational behaviour — through the breaking down of traditional or theoretical frameworks, and, more broadly, world consciousness in transitions; or
- a reflection of the inherently paradoxical nature of leadership and of human existence itself.

This chapter will review the notion of paradox in leadership theory and practice, and will explore some of the seeming incongruities, tensions and paradoxes within the emergent-leadership paradigms of the West. The chapter will conclude with a few reflections on the future of leadership theory, taking into consideration the incongruities, tensions and paradoxes identified therein.

Notion of paradox within leadership theory and practice

Hofstede (1994: 9–10), the doyen of cross-cultural research on management, sees a fundamental distinction between Eastern thinking (represented by, for example, Confucianism, Buddhism and Hinduism) and Western thinking (dominant in the Judaeo-Christian-Muslim intellectual tradition) as being:

> In the East, a qualification does not exclude its opposite, which is an essential element of Western logic . . . Thus in the East the search for truth is irrelevant, because there is no need for a single and absolute truth and the assumption that a person can possess an objective truth is absent. Instead . . . expressing a concern for virtue: for proper ways of living (like, practising perseverance and thrift, or respecting tradition and social obligations) which is less obvious in the West where virtue tends to be derived from truth.

Thus, although a recognition of paradox and incongruities may open up directions for future thought on leadership, it may also fall into the Western trap of trying to solve the irreconcilable rather than recognizing or valuing paradox as a feature of human existence. Increasingly, theorists on leadership and organizational behaviour do appear to be recognizing paradox and 'speaking the unspeakable' about human behaviour. Stacey's (1996) views on the informal 'shadow' side of the organization being its source of double-loop creativity and learning (that is, learning which challenges and modifies existing norms, procedures, policies and objectives), as well as a growing body of literature on irrational, 'deviant', emotional aspects of organizations and people (Pascale, 1990; Fineman, 1993) are cases in point.

It would be equally remiss, however, not to recognize transitions in Western paradigms and to consider the effect thereof on creating potentially conflicting paradigms within leadership thought. Some of the significant influences shaping changing leadership thought appear to include the interrelated impacts of:

1. *Changing world circumstances* (including the emergence of a global world, increasing cultural diversity within nations and the changing gender composition of work);

2. *Changing ways of looking at the world* (including the influences of postmodernism, the 'new sciences' and incrementalist views of strategy). Postmodernism, in particular, through positing the existence of multiple 'realities' rather than the existence of 'one truth', increasingly challenges literal-metaphorical, real-unreal and rational-irrational dualities. Complexity and chaos theories — the 'new sciences' — likewise challenge Newtonian assumptions of an ordered world in which foresight and human agency are the order of the day. Incrementalist views on strategy (such as Mintzberg's (1994) 'emergent' model of strategy) similarly challenge the concept of a leader who formulates a clear vision towards which the organization's actions are orchestrated. Incrementalists view the strategy formulation process rather as a form of 'muddling along' in which a vision, often only recognizable as such in hindsight, emerges through the actions of the organizational collective rather than as the result of a 'grand plan' formulated by an individual strategist (Whittington, 1993); and,

3. *Changing world needs and consciousness*. In respect of the latter, a self-organizing earth consciousness akin to the Gaia principle may be influencing Western consciousness to unite masculine and feminine, yang and yin, principles to address the 'wicked' (that is, complex, systemic and paradoxical) problems confronting the earth.

Figure 9.1 (taken from Hill, 1998) identifies some current incongruities, tensions and paradoxes in leadership thought and practice.

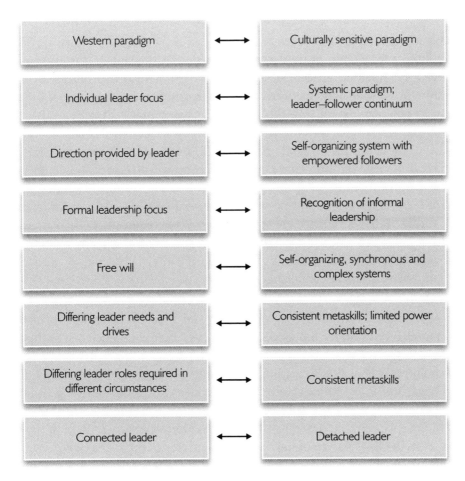

Western paradigm	Culturally sensitive paradigm
Individual leader focus	Systemic paradigm; leader–follower continuum
Direction provided by leader	Self-organizing system with empowered followers
Formal leadership focus	Recognition of informal leadership
Free will	Self-organizing, synchronous and complex systems
Differing leader needs and drives	Consistent metaskills; limited power orientation
Differing leader roles required in different circumstances	Consistent metaskills
Connected leader	Detached leader

Figure 9.1
Incongruities, tensions and paradoxes in the emerging leadership paradigm
(Taken from Hill, 1998)

Western conceptions vs. emerging leadership paradigms

A paradox or incongruity underlying many of the dualisms identified in Figure 9.1 appears to relate to the strongly Western roots of current literature on leadership, and the seeming incompatibility between these roots and the mental models consistent with an emerging complexity and chaos paradigm. At a fundamental level, literature on organizations may without much challenge be characterized as (to use the terminology of Boyacigiller and Adler, 1991) a 'parochial dinosaur' derived from and implicitly representing primarily North American cultural assumptions. The concept of 'leadership', in its entirety or in respect of the form it assumes, may be a peculiarly Western construct. There is currently a paucity of cross-cultural research on leadership, and much of that which has occurred has appeared to take the cross-cultural validity of the existence of the concept for granted and rather test the applicability of Western forms of leadership to 'foreign' cultures.

Whittington (1993), however, warns against accepting Anglo-Saxon conceptualizations of leadership as universal. He posits that the French, for example, do not have a term equating to leadership (1993: 48). Cross-cultural research into leadership, such that it is, has certainly challenged the normative (prescriptive) models of leadership posed through the decades by primarily American theorists. Hui Hai (Blofeld, 1962), by way of illustration, describes two fundamental features of 'Chinese familism' as (1) paternalism, implying a strong acceptance of hierarchical power relations, and (2) the tendency to categorize individuals into either an in-group or an out-group. Cultural values of this nature suggest a very different form of leadership to that advocated within a Western frame of reference where values of individualism, a low acceptance of power distances between members (that is, a low acceptance of strongly hierarchical power relationships between members of the cultural group) and an internalization of 'masculine' values of assertiveness and challenge are the norm (Hofstede, 1994).

The dominant logic of the bulk of organizational behaviour literature confers a strong role to the human agent in planning and directing her or his future. The mental models of Western 'individualist' cultures tend to be structured around the individual, whereas cognition in 'collectivist' cultures tend to centre on the group as the subject of analysis. According to Gaddis (1997), combined notions of the world being linear, evolutionary and progressive created ideal fertile grounds in which to plant the seeds of future-oriented planning. The Enlightenment tradition of the eighteenth century contributed to these notions through spawning the concept of a 'progressive theory of history' in which 'we were assured that purposeful humans are capable of achieving longer-term improvement in their social, political and economic institutions' (1997: 39). Management literature, particularly until the 1980s and 1990s, propagated a similar view of the efficacy of human agency, with managers being expected to plan, organize, lead and control by writers of the classical school (Gibson, Ivancevich, and Donnelly, 1988). These notions of the modality of human existence are strongly compatible with a 'heroic' view of the leader as an individual who, normally from a formally recognized position of power, directs the actions of others towards a desired future.

The assumptions of individual agency, free will and formal sources of authority still implicit within much of leadership literature and practice appear particularly at odds with the emerging new-science paradigm. In particular, a key incongruity appears to be the continued emphasis on the role of *the* leader — little attention is given to the roles required by the other players in the interaction for its effectiveness. The assumption inherent in labelling certain people as 'leaders' suggests that leadership, rather than followership, is the dominant role for certain individuals in all spheres of their lives. Although a leader–follower continuum is mentioned by a number of authors (for example, Barnes and Kriger, 1986;

Mindell, 1992; and Townsend and Gebhart, 1997), this area appears little developed.

A continued focus on single leaders and an assumption of static leader–follower status seems particularly surprising and incongruous in a systems paradigm which gives its attention to the totality of the system in creating organizational effectiveness, and gives recognition to the vital role of collectives and informal structures within an organization. Likewise, preserving the role of vision formulation and articulation as the domain of the leader (Gilliland, Tynan and Smith, 1996; and Bennis, 1994a, for example) appears unnecessarily prescriptive from a systems perspective — should not the vision emerge from group interaction? Those authors who do recognize a role for informal leadership within an organization, often appear to present an untextured understanding of the difficulties of realizing such roles in mechanistic, hierarchical organizations. As many people who have tried to play informal leadership roles (influencing from 'below') will recognize, a power structure in which status and positional power wield strong influence can strongly undermine informal leadership roles that potentially alter or undermine the paradigm of the dominant power group. Those individuals who pose a challenge to the status quo may, rather than being appreciated as a potential source of innovation and as breathing new life into stagnant organizations, be labelled as 'maverick' or 'deviant' and suffer personally in terms of belittlement, backlash or exclusion from the 'inner core' of the organization. For informal leadership to be allowed to play an effective role, the constructs of hierarchy and consequently positional power would seem to need to be fundamentally dislodged from traditional mental models. This presents a tremendous challenge for leaders who wish to assume roles consistent with the emergent paradigm.

To fully recognize the role of groups and informal structures in a leadership process may entail, aside from a paradigmatic change, a *tremendous amount of courage* on the part of current leaders to relinquish the individual status and prestige an individualistic formal notion of 'leadership' confers on them. Research by Stacey (1991) suggests that although the majority of managers possess explicit models of the strategy process which accord with classical assumptions, in practice implicit models more akin to incrementalism guide the real strategic development and control of their businesses. A tension between implicit and explicit models may threaten not only the mental model of the leader who begins to doubt the dominant logic of human agency, but also the self-esteem of the leader who, steeped in this logic, believes that he or she is incapable of effecting the influence he or she should have on the world. The potential loss of self-esteem may be particularly painful to leaders, who are likely to comprise a high proportion of individuals who are power- or achievement-motivated. According to Goleman (1997), psychological defence mechanisms such as repression, denial and reversal, projection, isolation, rationalization, sublimation, selective inattention and automatism will come into play where individuals need to mask 'simple truths with vital lies'. In order to preserve Western views that opposites cannot co-exist without dysfunctional conflict, leaders may engage in game playing or what Argyris (1990, in Stacey, 1996) terms 'organizational defence routines' to prevent them having to face up to what is really happening. For example, a leader in an organization experiencing rapid organizational cultural change may ascribe the cultural change to the initiatives of her or his 'transformation' team, rather than viewing cultural change as, perhaps, a confluence of changing societal values, and the wants, needs and actions of a variety of informal and formal players within the organization. In such organizational defence routines, the model likely to triumph is that which accords with the dominant logic, and hence narratives regarding individualistic, formal, directive leadership will be likely to be legitimated.

Paradox, incongruity and tension: the emerging model

Another paradox appears to be the emergence of a strongly normative model of effective leadership at a time when organizations are increasingly understood as complex phenomena (presumably requiring as complex and contextual a range of leadership processes and styles), and when cross-cultural research and postmodernist thought are encouraging a move away from 'one best way' modes of thought. Inherent in much of the leadership literature, particularly that of post-Greenleaf authors on 'servant-leadership', is a strongly normative model of the leader as reflexive, emotionally mature and strongly participative. Servant-leadership, as described in previous chapters, views the role of the leader as a steward or servant of her or his followers. Covey (1997: 3) describes the stewardship that servant-leadership entails in the following manner: ' . . . we may give up not only material things but also the price and arrogance of *me* and *mine* in exchange for a humble heart and a contrite spirit, for an ethic of service and sacrifice.'

The paradox or incongruity herein, lies in the assumption that, despite differing needs and drives among leaders, effective leaders either possess or can develop a fairly consistent meta-outlook on life (including a deep humanity, strong humility and a principled orientation). This appears to assume that, despite leader divergence in motivation (for example along McClelland's 1962, power, achievement and social orientations), strong status or power orientations will no longer play a role among leaders of the future. If an individualistic power orientation is a product of socialization, all well and good. But if, rather, it represents a more inherent personality trait (as posited by McClelland, 1962) it is more likely to play a role among leaders, particularly in the West where this theory was developed.

Cursory mention is made in some of the literature of the requirement for leaders to play changing roles, as necessitated by differing requirements and spirits (roles or emotions that may be present) of the situation (Mindell, 1992; Melrose, 1996; Goleman, 1998), but few concrete examples of how this may be achieved are provided (perhaps 'The Enneagram' by Michael Goldberg is a first step to a workable model), nor is the possibility of a strongly autocratic leadership style being effective in certain circumstances opened up for debate. It is further assumed that effective leaders can manage the paradox of needing to be simultaneously connected and detached from the followers and the presenting circumstances (Mindell, 1992; Melrose, 1996) — a considerable challenge indeed. It may therefore be questioned whether the emerging 'servant-leader' model in fact liberates good leaders, through allowing them to act as integrated individuals able to inject soul and meaning into the workplace, or whether it presents yet another normative model of leadership unattuned to the complexities of differing circumstances and organizations — thereby functioning as a 'straightjacket' into which leaders, irrespective of background, motivation and personality, are required to fit. In fact, we need to question whether the emerging leadership paradigms do not eulogize individualistic models of leadership more so than the paradigms of the past.

Observation of a number of South African business leaders bears out this paradox, with a few leaders experiencing or evidencing a high degree of tension between a 'requirement' to follow a participative servant-leader model, whilst experiencing an internal desire to play more autocratic roles at times, and evidencing individualistic views on leadership with themselves as 'leaders' sharply in the foreground and 'followers' in relief. As a starting point, a tremendous divergence in outlook and conceptualization of the role of leader is evident among South African business leaders. For example, the CEO of a leading company, in a presentation to the 1998 University of Cape Town MBA class, appeared to hold a fairly individualistic view on leadership, with himself as 'leader' sharply in the foreground, and 'followers' in relief. His discourse suggested a strong separation between 'management/leadership' and 'employees', some instrumentalism in terms of the need for participative process, and a fairly planned — rather than emergent — approach to strategy. On the other end of the spectrum were a number of leaders, whom I have interviewed from within social development organizations (formerly termed 'welfare' organizations). In an interview with a leader from St. Luke's Hospice, for example, she referred to the volunteers and employees of the branch she had founded as 'us' and 'we' throughout the interview, and she appeared to not separate the branch into 'leaders' and 'the led' when she was asked whether she experienced any management or leadership difficulties or challenges in the branch. In addition, she seemed to be an emergent strategist who 'feels the vision' deeply and imbues the vision within her field, rather than consciously articulating it.

Incongruities were also evident within individual leaders. The CEO mentioned above, for example, demonstrated ambivalence between democratic and autocratic leadership processes, being as he described himself, 'an iron fist in a velvet glove'. Whereas this may reflect a leader's ability to change roles as needs alter, it may, alternatively, suggest that other personal motivations (such as a need for power or personal achievement) may play a role even within principle-driven leaders.

Leadership: reflections on the way ahead

Through reflection on a few of the incongruities, tensions and paradoxes of the emerging paradigm and in the field of leadership more broadly, it is suggested that the concept of leadership may need revisiting. Within a Western and, more particularly, Anglo-Saxon context, the term 'leadership' appears to carry many different definitions. The concept of leadership may need to be either:

1. broadened to integrate the notions of a constantly shifting leader–follower continuum (or a variety of 'leadership' roles that need to be assumed within a team or social system for it to function effectively) and the role of informal leaders; or

2. segmented into various subconcepts to allow more penetrative research into, and understanding of, what is currently a highly multifaceted concept.

Leadership theory needs to look beyond its peculiarly Western cultural and historical context, and the normative models such a context have produced, to embracing new and divergent world-views and making explicit the assumptions regarding human modality and leadership contained therein.

Despite the incongruities, tensions and paradoxes in leadership theory and practice which have been explored within this chapter, emerging leadership thought provides a potent source of inspiration for leaders wishing to play roles of personal integrity which seek to create 'a better world' through the empowerment of 'followers'. It also appears to hold greater promise for resolving the 'wicked', systemic problems confronting our world today and for producing a greater sense of humanity within Western work organizations.

Epilogue
The New Landscape

As adults, most of us have forgotten our original deep selves and the profound wisdom we possess. Except in rare moments of childlike spontaneity when we are exposed to something that touches us deeply, we forget that our selves have a knowing centre. We forget how to respond to what is within. We lose faith in ourselves and turn to external rules for guidance. The challenge is to regain that lost childlike spontaneity, tempered with adult's discipline, experience and wisdom — and constant humility. We must always be willing to test our 'inner truth' against its consequences in the outside world.

Zohar and Marshall, 2000

In looking to the future, we hope that you will use the themes presented in this book to reflect on what is really important and what leading means to you. The themes will inevitably raise new issues and trigger new questions. And these questions will then serve as triggers themselves of new experiences. And so the learning continues and the awareness broadens. We hope to have highlighted the fact that leadership is dynamic and complex, yet stable at the core and simple. The landscape in which we live has changed and is changing as we pass through. The old guidebook that told us what to look for and what to ignore is outdated. There are now new markers on the road; a different set of markers that don't tell us how much farther we have to go. Rather they point at things to reflect on, to ask questions about, so that we can ascertain for ourselves whether we're on the right track and doing the right things, or whether we are fooling ourselves. They don't necessarily bring clarity, but they relentlessly confront us with *the need to go inside* in order to transcend our own limitations and accept the awesome responsibility that *comes with leading*. They will remind us not to panic in the face of this lack of certainty about the future. They will make us conscious that paradox and ambiguity are ever-present realities that will define the leadership process in the twenty-first century. Here are the markers.

Followership

In an effort to clarify the ambiguous and complex concept of leadership, researchers and practitioners have followed many different paths that have each led to very different conclusions as to what exactly leadership is. Bass (in Van der Merwe, 1994: 235) lists a number of portrayals of leadership such as: the focus of group processes; a matter of personality; a matter of inducing compliance; the exercise of influence; a particular constellation of behaviours; a form of persuasion; a power relation; an instrument to achieve goals; an effect of interaction; a differentiated role; or the initiation of structure. Sometimes these various definitions have been combined. Hill (1998) makes the point that it is debatable whether these conceptualizations are competing or compatible; whether they represent a cluster of concepts or a multi-faceted concept; and whether or not they represent increasing accuracy in understanding leadership or the changing nature of leadership itself over the decades. However, as disparate as they are, these definitions have in common the notion of a force that influences followers in a particular activity. There is nothing to suggest that this common element will, in the future, disappear from the repertoire of leaders.

Leadership and followership are inexorably linked. Leaders have a good story to tell and followers buy into it. Leadership and followership are on the same continuum, along which we move constantly: a follower one moment and a leader the next. And, just as much as leadership doesn't necessarily mean dictating people's moves, followership does not imply a passive acceptance of leadership. Ideally there is an active and dynamic engagement between the leader and his or her followers. Good leaders invite and encourage such engagement. Gardner (1990) describes the best leaders as those with a strong sense of mission, who are active instead of reactive, shaping ideas instead of responding to them. They have a good story to tell which they can communicate in ways that resonate with their followers, because they embody the essence of their story in their daily lives. Nelson Mandela's story is that of a rainbow nation — nation-building through recognition of cultural pluralism and diversity. President Thabo Mbeki, his successor, tells a story of an African Renaissance — the rebirth of Africa, in which the continent recovers as a whole, economically, socially, technologically and politically. When we have the capacity to tell such stories and rally people around us to live out this story . . . that is when we play a leadership role. And when we buy in to other people's stories, we become followers.

In this time of constant flux and rapid change, each of us will be required to exercise and develop our talents to lead and to follow. This is an awesome responsibility, because the potential for abuse by ruthless leaders and by colluding followers is always there — such is human nature. When we hand over all power and authority to one or more central figures, we relinquish the possibility to determine the direction and shape of our future. Such leadership, and such followership, preserve the unchecked exercise of power and perpetuates dependency.

Openness and authenticity

As tomorrow's leaders, we will have to be committed to a kind of humility that we do not always associate with people in power. We need to find the problem to address rather than the person to blame. We need to take error and failure in stride, as experiences to teach us because, as Toynbee (1992) observed, 'nothing fails like success'. Besides, yesterday's success does not help us deal with today's new chal-lenge. We will need to be open to possibilities and create a culture in which ideas that are fuelled by passion can emerge unhampered by fear. As leaders, we can do this by setting a personal example and by acting out, and living, the very qualities we espouse. This requires an openness and a vulnerability that can only be rooted in a strong sense of self. A confidence that, being ourselves, and remaining true to our purpose, vision, and principles, is the best strategy, even if it is not always the easiest, the most popular or the strategy with the biggest rewards. Eysenck (1972) informs us that

> ... the notion of rational man, acting in conformity with reason and knowledge and guided entirely by his brain, is erroneous, although still widespread and still governs many of our educational and social policies. Instead, ... much of human conduct is governed by heart rather than by head; by emotion, rather than by reason.

This knowledge will free us, as Covey (1995) suggests '[to] start living more out of [our] imagination than [our] memory'. Martin Buber, in *The Way of Man*, reminds us that every man's foremost task is the actualization of his unique unprecedented and never-recurring possibilities, and not the repetition of some-thing that another, be it even the greatest, has already achieved. 'To be no one but yourself in a world which is doing its best to make you just like everybody else, means to fight the greatest battle there is or ever will be' (ee cummings).

Passion

Leadership is fundamentally about tapping into people's passion.

> Passion is more honest than reason! To be sure, logic is more elegant, more sensible, and surely more prudent. And, one feels far more secure and calm with the rational. Pre-dictability never makes the heart race. Passion leaves a person feeling fearful of the 'on the edge', unanticipated outcome. It also makes us feel free, alive, and somehow 'a real, whole person'. And, when leaders surface that feeling in us, we are somehow more energized, more like a knight ready for battle.
>
> Bell, 1996: 13

This connection between passion and leadership has been articulated by the great philosophers all through the ages, and reiterated by our own contemporaries. Goethe reminds us to begin in boldness with whatever we can do, or dream we can do, because boldness has genius, power, and magic in it. Philosopher Hegel wrote: 'Nothing great in the world has been accomplished without passion.' Handy (1997: 14) tells us that 'a passion for the job provides the energy and focus that drive the organization and that acts as an example to others'. Passion creates a field of energy to which philosopher Rollo May refers when he writes: 'There is an energy field between humans. And, when a person reaches out in passion, it is usually met with an answering passion.' Memorable and effective leaders are those who have discovered their own, authentic passion and energy, and can thus operate from that base with resilience and boldness. *The leadership we seek lies within each of us.* 'Many people feel called to a vocation by an inner prompting. The idea of being called does not mean that a person is being singled out for a special mission, only that there is a special resonance in one's life that will find its fullest expression and connection with a larger whole within the context of which one is feeling called' (Spangler, 1996: 48). Howard Gardner, in his book, *Leading Minds: An Anatomy of Leadership*, celebrates the lives of Mahatma Gandhi and Jean Monnet. Gardner (1995: 278) states 'for both Monnet and Gandhi, in the deepest sense, their methods were their message'. They became conscious of deep universal truths regarding global cooperation and the nature of being. They repeated these truths quietly and persistently to all who would listen until these truths were widely accepted.

Complexity and ambiguity

The future calls for leaders who are willing to live and work within the context of complexity, uncertainty, ambiguity. White, Hodgson and Crainer (1996: 143) write about 'white-water leadership' and stress the need for future leaders to be able to cope with uncertainty and turbulence. They claim that the first thing a leader has to learn to do differently is to move towards uncertainty rather than away from it, a seemingly counter-intuitive move. They list five critical aspects of white water leadership, each raising a number of questions, as prerequisites of living purposely and productively in this new turbulent world.

1. *Difficult learning:* How many of you can honestly say that you work for organizations in which risk taking is positively encouraged? How many of you admit to your own mistakes? How many of you actively and deliberately learn from them?

2. *Maximizing energy:* How many of you channel your own, and other people's energies effectively? What gives you energy and pleasure? Are you able to enthuse others to believe in their own potential?

3. *Resonant simplicity:* How much resonance do you achieve in your organization? Do you inspire others by simplifying the complex?

4. *Multiple focus:* How focused are you in the short term? How focused are you on the long term? How can the two be balanced effectively to the benefit of the individual and the organization?

5. *Mastering inner sense:* How often do you follow your intuitive judgement — and admit to it? How do you encourage others to do the same?

These questions are asked so as to remind us that, contrary to the public image of the leader who has all the answers and simplifies our lives, leaders should ask questions and help those of us who choose to follow to see the complexity around us, and learn to live with the ambiguity inherent in complex living systems.

Organizational conversations

In healthy organizations people talk with one another. They learn from one another in ongoing dialogue as they do their work. People tell stories and ask questions. They exchange jokes and 'hang out' together as they discuss their problems. People get advice and coaching from a colleague. They ask for help with sticky business problems through the company e-mail and Intranet. They make unique contributions and commit to action because they are connected to each other in relationships they value. These informal threads of conversation are as much a core business process as the distribution process or the marketing plan or the product development process. Good leaders know that good conversations around questions that matter is a core process for building the organizational intelligence which enables other business processes to create results.

But how many organizations consider conversation to be the heart of the 'real work' of knowledge creation and building of intellectual capital? We would like to challenge executives and employees to consider a time, in either their personal or professional lives, when they had a really good conversation. What were the qualities that made it worthwhile? What enabled that conversation to be productive and useful? How did you feel about yourself, during and after the conversation? How did the other person, persons or group react to the conversation? How did they behave subsequent to having the conversation?

At the Graduate School of Business of the University of Cape Town we posed those questions to members of a junior management development programme, and, while there was a wide range of individual experience, there were a few common themes: 'There was a sense of mutual respect between us.' 'We took the time to talk together and reflect about what we each thought was important.' 'It strengthened our mutual commitment.' 'We listened to each other, even if there were differences.' 'I was accepted and not judged by the other person.' 'We talked about things that really mattered.' 'We discovered shared understanding that wasn't there when we began this course.' 'The conversation helped build our relationship.' 'This sort of conversation doesn't happen often enough.' However, in the past and still currently, employees, followers, students, and family members have been told to 'stop talking and get on with the task'. There is a common and generally disparaging expression in our Western culture which condemns a person or a group for being 'all talk and no action'. We are discovering that it is actually the talking, the networking of conversations, that determines the action. The tenets of the new leadership paradigm suggest that a more useful frame of reference might be to 'start talking to do the task'; an appropriate process will lead to an effective outcome.

Storytelling

Understanding knowledge creation as a process of making tacit knowledge explicit — a matter of metaphors, analogies, and models — has direct implications for how a company designs its organization and defines leadership roles and respon-sibilities within it. 'Effective leaders put words to the formless longings and deeply felt needs of others. They create communities out of words. They tell stories that capture minds and win hearts' (Bennis, 1996). Through these stories we discover who cares about what, and who will take accountability for next steps. Gardner (1995: 14) says about leadership: 'The ultimate impact of the leader depends most significantly on the particular story that he or she relates or embodies, and the reception to that story.' He describes the characteristics of an effective story as one that must compete with others and transplant, suppress, complement or out-measure other stories. Colin Hall talks about creating 'rich pictures', for those who are willing to follow (April, 1997). Khanya Motshabi, chief operating officer of Future Growth in South Africa and friend of one of the authors, sees a leader's role as that of one who simplifies, symbolizes, and sloganizes strategy. The story needs to have a dynamic perspective that addresses both individual and group identities and helps group members to frame future options as circumstances change.

The greater the diversity of people, ideas, backgrounds, experiences, insights, qualifications, the richer the story-picture becomes. Diversity is primarily about the realities that each one of us experiences. Reality is a social construct. We create it by paying attention to some things and not to others, by valuing some things and not others. We can construct reality together by reflecting on, by telling sto-ries of, such things together. Wheatley (1998: 340) tells us that 'as individuals telling our stories to one another, we create an interpretation of our lives, their purpose and significance. And through shared stories, we see patterns emerge that unite our separating experiences into shared meanings.' We encourage you to *tell your story* and *listen to the stories of others*. Often storytelling forces individuals to dig deep inside themselves. Consequently, Covey (1999) terms this process the 'inside-out approach'. He informs us that the inside-out approach usually requires sacrifice of pride and ego. All four unique human gifts or endowments — self-awareness, imagination, conscience, and independent will — are usually exer-cised and magnified. 'Almost always,' we are told by Covey (1999: xix), 'there's a vision of what's possible and desirable. And almost always, marvelous things result. Trust is restored. Broken relationships are redeemed. Personal moral author-ity to continue the upward change effort is evident.'

Vision and values

Wheatley (1999) talks about the fractal organization where a few guiding princi-ples or values shape behaviour. We can see the same kind of behaviour at every level of the organization, because it has been patterned into the organization from the very start. Information in a fractal organization is like solar energy, nourish-ing the vision and the values and allowing them to develop as the organization and its workers develop. As more and more people come into contact with each other in organizations, more and new relationships are formed, and new fields of energy are created. Unrestricted information and wide participation will allow the wisdom of each person, each division, to blend and to create new information, new stories, new visions. Information has the tendency to amplify when shared, allowing different interpretations to interact, add a new slant, reveal as well as create increasing complexity. This and other flows of information allow organizational knowledge to be organized into ever-changing, expanding and contracting forms.

This is the disequilibrium Stacey (1995) sees as the prerequisite for the growth of new structures. Current structures need to dissipate in order to arrive at new ones. Structures in organizations are thus only temporary solutions to facilitate, rather than interfere with the process. Leaders of the future need to relinquish the illusion of control and allow the natural, inherent order to emerge instead. They can do this if they dare, and if they are willing to trust their workers. By being sincere and by walking their talk, that is, by living the values that they espouse, they establish their credibility and are able to lead from values and vision, rather than from their formal authority.

Relationships

Quantum physics, through observations of subatomic particles, teaches us that particles come into being only through interaction with another energy source. Electrons and photons, mesons and nucleons change from position to momentum, from particles to waves, from mass to energy, all in response to each other and to their environment. Nothing exists or is observable in a subatomic world without encountering something else — relationships are all there is to reality.

> If one is leading, teaching, dealing with young people or engaged in any other activity that involves influencing, directing, guiding, helping or nurturing, the whole tone of the relationship is conditioned by one's faith in human possibilities. That is the generative element, the source of the current that gives life to the relationship.
>
> *Gardner, 1990: 199*

No work can be sustained without attention to the relationships that support it. In fact, *nurturing those relationship is the real work*. Intuitively we know this, but our rational mind dismisses relation work as 'soft' and a waste of time. Emphasizing the relational aspects of leadership is a central theme for any organization functioning in the new paradigm.

Letting go

> Each of us has the right and the responsibility to assess the roads which lie ahead, and those over which we have travelled. And if the future road looms ominous or unpromising, and the roads back inviting, then we need to gather our resolve and, carrying only the necessary baggage, step off that road into another direction. If the

new choice is also impalatible, without embarrassment, we must be ready to change that as well.

Maya Angelou, American poet and writer

Naidoo (1998: 10) reminds us that 'good leadership is not something to possess; it is something to give — an expression of one's self'. The more we try to hold on to something, the more likely we are to lose it. In this age of rapid change and frequent transformation, progress cannot be made until we let go of what we are holding onto. We must see the chains that bind us to our past and that prevent us from understanding who we really are. Only then can we let go of them, freeing us to move on to try something else, to gain more understanding of who we are. But letting go is not just about the past. It also applies to letting go of specific outcomes, an investment in specific results that have to be attained at all costs. This is what led to the tragedy of the space craft, Challenger, and countless other ones. Fromm (1956) argues that, for the first time in history, the physical survival of the human race depends on a radical change of the human heart. 'This is a call to service that will take great courage — to leave what we have and move out, not without fear, but without succumbing to that fear. It is a call to redefine what is possible, to see a vision of a new world and to be willing to undertake, step by step, what is necessary in concrete terms to achieve that vision' (Jaworski, 1996: 57).

Awareness

We finish the book by returning to the place were we began, because we believe that *fundamental to the exercise of leadership is awareness*. No matter the people, the culture, or the context. As leaders we have to think and know with everything we have. To borrow from Walt Whitman: 'Leaders are people large enough to contain multitudes.' Exploring what it means to be aware, we have to re-learn how to be fully present in each moment, much like infants are.

> The present moment is the most profound and challenging teacher we will ever meet in our lives. It is a compassionate teacher, it extends to us no judgement, no censure, no measurement of success and failure. The present moment is a mirror, and in its reflection we learn how to see.

Kornfield and Feldman, 1996: 179

We encourage you, the reader, to look into this mirror with curiosity and humility to see what contributes to the confusion and discord in your life, and what contributes to harmony and understanding. You will see what it is that connects you with others, and what alienates you or sets you apart. Taking a hard look into the mirror is like listening inwardly and finding out what you need to let go of and what you need to develop. Being aware is a fundamental mode of existence in the world, a prerequisite for aliveness, for authentic self-expression and authentic relationships.

The old and the new: comfort in confusion

We hope that this book will have delighted you, challenged you, annoyed you, confused you, surprised you, made you feel lighter here, heavier there, stronger, hopeful and encouraged. We also hope that this book invites you to continue to explore yourself and others, read beyond your technical or professional domain, re-read old classics and reflect on the journey you have taken so far, and where it is taking you. We have synthesized that which countless people have said before us, recently or ages ago. This is wisdom that is as new as the times we live in, and as old as the timeless messages that are carried by all the great religious traditions. This book is essentially about the infinite possibilities of the self. This book is also about leaving your comfort zone and entering a complex, challenging, exciting and confusing place. We hope that you can become comfortable with the confusion of the Broken Images, evoked so poignantly by David Jones (1997) in his poem of the same title:

> He is quick, thinking in clear images;
> I am slow, thinking in broken images.
>
> He becomes dull, trusting to his clear images;
> I become sharp, mistrusting my broken images.
>
> Trusting his images he assumes their relevance;
> Mistrusting my images I question their relevance.
>
> Assuming their relevance he assumes the fact;
> Questioning their relevance I question the fact.
>
> When the fact fails him he questions his senses;
> When the fact fails me I approve my senses.
>
> He continues quick and dull in his clear images;
> I continue slow and sharp in my broken images.
>
> He in a new confusion of his understanding;
> I in a new understanding of my confusion.

Bibliography

Ackoff, R.L. (1994). *The Democratic Corporation*. New York: Oxford University Press.

Ackoff, R.L. (1984). Mechanisms, Organisms, and Social Systems, *Strategic Management Journal* **5**.

Adair, J. (1990). *Not Bosses But Leaders* (2 ed.). Surrey: Kogan Page.

Ansoff, I. (1965). *Corporate Strategy*. Harmondsworth: Penguin.

April, K.A. (1999). Leading through communication, conversation and dialogue. *Leadership & Organization Development Journal* **20** (5), pp. 231–241.

April, K.A. (1997). *An Investigation into the Applicability of New Science, Chaos Theory, and Complexity Theory to Leadership, and Development of Guiding Principles for the Modern Leader and Organization*. (MBA Dissertation, Graduate School of Business, University of Cape Town, South Africa).

Argyris, C. (1999). *On Organizational Learning* (2 ed.). Oxford: Blackwell

Argyris, C. (July–August 1994). Good communication that blocks learning. *Harvard Business Review*, pp. 77–85.

Argyris, C. (1993). *Knowledge for Action: A Guide to Overcoming Barriers to Organizational Change*. San Francisco: Jossey-Bass.

Argyris, C. (1990). *Overcoming Organizational Defenses: Facilitating Organizational Learning*. Boston: Allyn and Bacon.

Argyris, C. (1985). Making knowledge more relevant to practice: Maps for action. In: E.E. Lawler III, A.M. Mohrman, Jr., S.A Mohrman, G.E. Ledford, and T.G. Cummings & Associates. *Doing Research that is Useful for Theory and Practice*. San Francisco: Jossey-Bass, pp. 79–106.

Argyris, C. (1982). *Reasoning, Learning and Action: Individual and Organizational*. San Francisco: Jossey-Bass.

Argyris, C. and Schön, D. (1978). *Organizational Learning: A Theory of Action Perspective*. Reading, MA.: Addison-Wesley.

Autry, J. (1992). *Love and Profit: The Art of Caring Leadership*. New York: Avon Business Books.

Baker Miller, J. (1986). *Toward a New Psychology of Women*. Boston: Bacon Press.

Banet, A.G. Jr. (1976). Yin/Yang: A perspective on theories of group development. In: *1976 Annual Handbook of Group Facilitators*. San Francisco: University Associates.

Banner, D.K. and Gagné, T.E. (1995). *Designing Effective Organizations: Traditional & Transformational Views.* London: Sage Publications.

Barciela, S. (1998). Dharamshala dreaming: A traveller's search for the meaning of work. In: L. Spears (Ed.). *Insights on Leadership: Service, Stewardship, Spirit, and Servant-Leadership.* New York: John Wiley & Sons, pp. 96–115.

Barclay, J. (1996). Assessing the benefits of learning logs. *Education & Training* **38** (2), pp. 30–38.

Barnes, L.B. and Kriger, M.P. (Fall 1986). The hidden side of organizational leadership. *Sloan Management Review,* pp. 15–25.

Bass, B.M. (1990). *Handbook of Leadership.* New York: Free Press.

Bass, B. and Avolio, B.J. (1992). Developing transformational leadership — 1992 and beyond. *Journal of European Industrial Training* **14** (5), pp. 21–27.

Beckard, R. and Pritchard, W. (1992). *Changing the Essence: The Art of Creating and Leading Fundamental Change in Organizations.* San Francisco, CA: Jossey-Bass.

Beerel, A. (1998). *Leadership Through Strategic Planning.* London: International Thomson Business Press.

Belasco, J.A. and Stayer, R.C. (1993). *Flight of the Buffalo.* New York: Warner Books.

Bell, C.R. (October 1996). The leader's greatest gift. *Executive Excellence* **13** (10), pp. 13–14.

Bennis, W. (October 1996). Leader as transformer. *Executive Excellence* **13** (10), pp. 15–16.

Bennis, W. (1994a). Introducing change. *Executive Excellence* **11** (11), pp. 9–10.

Bennis, W. (1994b). *On Becoming a Leader.* Boston: Addison-Wesley.

Bennis, W. (1993a). Learning some basic truisms about leadership. In: M. Ray and A. Rinzler (Eds.). *The New Paradigm in Business. Emerging Strategies for Leadership and Organizational Change.* New York: Putnam Publishing Group.

Bennis, W. (1993b). Why leaders can't lead. In: J.L. Pierce and J.W. Newstrom (Eds.). *The Manager's Bookshelf: A Mosaic of Contemporary Views* (3 ed.). New York: HarperCollins College Publishers, pp. 165–172.

Bennis, W. and Goldsmith, J. (1994). *Learning to Lead. A Workbook on becoming a Leader.* Reading, MA: Addison-Wesley.

Berger, P. and Luckmann, T. (1966). *The Social Construction of Reality.* New York: Anchor.

Bettis, R.A. and Prahalad, C.K. (1995). The dominant logic: Retrospective and extension. *Strategic Management Journal* **16**, pp. 5–14.

Bion, W.R. (1961). *Experiences in Groups,* New York: Basic Books.

Block, P. (1998). From leadership to citizenship. In: L. Spears (Ed.). *Insights on Leadership: Service, Stewardship, Spirit, and Servant-Leadership.* New York: John Wiley & Sons, pp. 87–95.

Block, P. (1993). *Stewardship.* San Francisco: Berret-Koehler Publishers.

Blofeld, J. (1962). *The Zen Teaching of Hui Hai on Sudden Illumination*. London: Rider.

Bohm, D. (1980). *Wholeness and the Implicate Order*. London: Ark Paperbacks.

Bolman, L.G. and Deal, T.E. (1991). *Reframing Organizations. Artistry, Choice, and Leadership*. San Francisco: Jossey-Bass.

Booysen, L. and Beaty, D.T. (December 1997). Linking transformation and change leadership in South Africa: A review of principles and practices. *SBL Research Review* **1** (1), pp. 9–18.

Boyacigiller, N.A. and Adler, N. (1991). The parochial dinosaur: Organizational science in a global context. *Academy of Management Review* 16 (2), pp. 262–290.

Bridges, W. (1980). *Transitions: Making Sense of Life's Changes*. Reading, MA: Addison, Wesley, Longman.

Brockman, H. (1998). *Integrative Healing Technologies*. URL address: http://www.cyberis.net/~hbrock/session.htm.

Brown, J. S. and Duguid, P. (1986). Organizational learning and communities-of-practice: Toward a unified view of working, learning and innovation. *Organizational Science* **32** (5), pp. 554–571.

Burrell, G. (1992). Back to the future: Time and organization. In: M. Reed and M. Hughes (Eds.). *Rethinking Organization: New Directions in Organization Theory and Analysis*. London: Sage.

Butler, J. (1994). From action to thought: The fulfilment of human potential. In: J. Edwards (Ed.). *Thinking: International Interdisciplinary Perspectives*. Melbourne: Hawker Brownlow Education.

Campbell, J. (1949). *The Hero with a Thousand Faces*. New York: MJF Books.

Capra, F. (1996). *The Web of Life: A New Scientific Understanding of Living Systems*. New York: Anchor Books.

Carrell, M.R., Jennings, D.F. and Hearin, C. (1997). *Fundamentals of Organizational Behaviour*. Englewood Cliffs, NJ: Prentice-Hall.

Cashman, K. (1998). *Leadership from the Inside Out: Becoming a Leader for Life*. Provo, Utah: Executive Excellence Publishing.

Catford, L. and Ray, M. (1991). *The Path of the Everyday Hero*. New York: G.P. Putnam's Sons.

Chambers, R. (1997). *Whose Reality Counts: Putting the First Last*. London: Intermediate Technology Publications.

Cleveland, H. (1997). *Leadership and the Information Revolution*. (Paper of The World Academy of Arts and Science and International Leadership Academy of the United nations University, Minneapolis).

Cohen, M.D., March, J.D. and Olsen, J.P. (1972). A garbage can model of organizational choice. *Administrative Science Quarterly* **17**, pp. 1–25.

Conger, J.A. (Summary prepared by Jim Laumeyer) (1993). The charismatic leader. In: J.L. Pierce and J.W. Newstrom (Eds.). *The Manager's Bookshelf: A*

Mosaic of Contemporary Views (3 ed.). New York: HarperCollins College Publishers, pp. 181–184.

Coulson-Thomas, C. (1997). *The Future of the Organization: Achieving Excellence Through Business Transformation*. London: Kogan Page

Covey, S.R. (1999). *Living the 7 Habits: Stories of Change and Inspiration*. New York: Simon & Schuster.

Covey, S.R. (1997). Sense of stewardship. *Executive Excellence* **14** (7), p. 3.

Covey, S.R. (October 1996). High wire, no net. *Executive Excellence* **13** (10), pp. 3–4.

Covey, S.R. (1995). Conscientious change. *Executive Excellence* **12** (2), p. 3.

Covey, S.R. (November 1994). New wine, old bottles. *Executive Excellence* **11** (12), pp. 3–4.

Covey, S.R. (1992). *Principle-Centered Leadership*. New York: Simon & Schuster.

Covey, S.R. (1989). *The Seven Habits of Highly Effective People*, New York: Simon & Schuster.

Covey, S.R., Merrill, A.R. and Merrill, R.R. (1994). *First Things First*. London: Simon & Schuster.

Daudelin, M. (Winter 1996). Learning from experience through reflection. *Organizational Dynamics*, pp. 36–48.

Davenport, T.H. and Prusak, L. (1998). *Working Knowledge: How Organizations Manage What They Know*. Boston, MA: Harvard Business School Press.

De Board, R. (1978). *The Psychoanalysis of Organizations*. London: Tavistock.

De Pree, M. (1989). *Leadership is an Art*. New York: Dell Publishing Division.

Dixon, N.M. (1998). *Dialogue at Work*. London: Lemos & Krane.

Dodgson, M. (1993). Organizational learning: A review of some literatures. *Organizational Studies* **14** (3), pp. 375–393.

Dowling, C. (1990). *Cinderella Complex: Women's Hidden Fear of Independence*. New York: Summit Books.

Erickson, M.J. (1985). *Christian Theology*. Grand Rapids: Baker Book House.

Evans, L. (1999). *Diversity: Being Different Together.* (Unpublished working paper, Strategic Learning Web).

Eysenck, H.J. (1972). *Psychology is About People*. London: Allen Lane.

Fadiman, A. (1997). *The Spirit Catches You and You Fall Down*. New York: Farrar, Straus and Giroux.

Farr, J. N. (January 1995). Changing minds. *Executive Excellence* **12** (1), pp. 5–6.

Farson, R. (1996). *Management of the Absurd: Paradoxes of Leadership*. New York: Simon & Schuster.

Fiol, C. M. and Lyles, M. A. (1985). Organizational learning. *Academy of Management Review* **10** (4), pp. 803–813.

Fineman, S. (1993). Organizations as emotional arenas. In: S. Fineman (Ed.). *Emotion in Organizations*. London: Sage Publications.

Firmage, G.J. (Ed.) (1994). *E.E. Cummings: Complete Poems 1904–1962*. New York: Liveright.

Ford, J. and Backoff, R. (1988). Organizational change in and out of dualities and paradox. In: R. Quinn and K. Cameron (Eds.). *Paradox and Transformation: Toward a Theory of Change in Organization and Management*. Cambridge, MA: Ballinger Publishing, pp. 81–121.

Ford, J.D. and Ford, L.W. (1995). The role of conversations in producing intentional change in organizations. *Academy of Management Review* **20** (3), pp. 541–570.

Fritz, R. (1984). *The Path of Least Resistance*. New York: Ballantine Books.

Fromm, E. (1956). *The Art of Loving*. New York: Harper and Row.

Gaddis, P.O. (1997). Strategy under attack. *Long Range Planning* **30** (1), pp. 38–45.

Gallwey, W.T. (1997). *The Inner Game of Tennis*. Random House.

Gardiner, J.J. (1998). Quiet presence: The holy ground of leadership. In: L. Spears (Ed.). *Insights on Leadership: Service, Stewardship, Spirit, and Servant-Leadership*. New York: John Wiley & Sons, pp. 116–125.

Gardner, H. (1995). *Leading Minds: An Anatomy of Leadership*. New York: Basic Books.

Gardner, J.W. (Summary prepared by James Meindl) (1993). On leadership. In: J.L. Pierce and J.W. Newstrom (Eds.). *The Manager's Bookshelf: A Mosaic of Contemporary Views* (3 ed.). New York: HarperCollins College Publishers, pp. 159–164.

Gardner, J.W. (1990). *On Leadership*. New York: The Free Press.

Gell-Mann, M. (1995). *The Quark and the Jaguar: Adventures in the Simple and the Complex*. New York: W.H. Freeman.

Gerard, G. and Teurfs, L. (August 1997). Dialogue and transformation. *Executive Excellence* **14** (8), pp. 16.

Gibson, E.D. (1998). *Servant Leadership*. (Working paper, Graduate School of Business, University of Cape Town).

Gibson, J.L., Ivancevich, J.M. and Donnelly, J.H. (1988). *Organizations* (6 ed.). Illinois: Irwin.

Giddens, A. (1994). *Beyond Left and Right — The Future of Radical Politics*. Stanford University Press.

Gilliland, M.W., Tynan, M. and Smith, K.L. (1996). *Leadership and Transformation in an Environment of Unpredictability*. (Working paper presented at the CAUSE annual conference).

Gleick, J. (1987). *Chaos: The Making of a New Science*. London: Heinemann.

Goldstein, J. (1994). *The Unshackled Organization: Facing the Challenge of Unpredictability through Spontaneous Reorganization*. New York: Productivity Pr.

Goleman, D. (1998). *Working with Emotional Intelligence*. London: Bloomsbury Publishing.

Goleman, D. (1997). *Vital Lies, Simple Truths: The Psychology of Self-Deception.* London: Bloomsbury Publishing.

Grantham, C.E. and Nichols, L.D. (1993). *The Digital Workplace: Designing Groupware Platforms*, New York: Van Nostrand Reinhold.

Greenberg, J. and Baron, R.B. (1993). *Behavior in Organizations: Understanding and Managing the Human Side of Work* (4 ed.). Boston: Allyn & Bacon.

Greenleaf, R. (1983). *Servant Leadership: A Journey into the Nature of Legitimate Power and Greatness.* Mahwah, NJ: Paulist Press.

Gull, G. (December 1994). In search of leadership. *Executive Excellence* **11** (12), p. 16.

Hamel, G. (July–August 1996). Strategy as revolution. *Harvard Business Review,* pp. 69–82.

Hamel, G. and Prahalad, C. (1994). *Competing for the Future.* Boston, MA: Harvard Business School Press.

Hamel, G. and Prahalad, C. (April 1993). Strategy as stretch and leverage. *Harvard Business Review.*

Handy, C. (1998). *Beyond Certainty: The Changing Worlds of Organizations.* Cambridge, MA: Harvard Business School Press.

Handy, C. (1997). New language of organizing. *Executive Excellence* **14** (5), pp. 13–14.

Handy, C. (1985). *Understanding Organizations.* Penguin Books Ltd.

Hax A.C. and Majluf, N.S. (1995). *Strategy Concept and Process: A Pragmatic Approach.* New York: Prentice-Hall.

Hedberg, B.L. (1981). How organizations learn and unlearn. In: P.C. Nystrom and W.H. Starbuck (Eds.). *Handbook of Organizational Design* I. New York: Oxford University Press, pp. 5–23.

Heider, J. (1986). *The Tao of Leadership: Leadership Strategies for a New Age.* New York: Bantam Books.

Heisenberg, W. (1958). *Physics and Philosophy.* New York: Harper Torchbooks.

Hersey, P. and Blanchard, K. (1982). *Management of Organizational Behaviour: Utilizing Human Resources*, Englewood Cliffs, NJ: Prentice-Hall.

Hill, S. (1998). *Leadership: A Personal Interpretation.* (Working paper, Graduate School of Business, University of Cape Town).

Hofstede, G. (1997). *Cultures and Organizations: Software of the Mind.* London: McGraw-Hill.

Hofstede, G. (1994). The business of international business is culture. *International Business Review* **3** (1), pp. 1–14.

Hofstede, G. (1980). *Culture's Consequences: International Differences in Work-Related Values.* Beverly Hills, CA: SAGE Publications.

Lewin, R. and Regine, B. (1999). *The Soul at Work: Unleashing the Power of Complexity Science for Business Success.* London: Orion.

Huber, G. P. (1991). Organizational learning: The contributing processes and the literatures. *Organizational Science* **2** (1), pp. 88–115.

Jaworski, J. (1998). Destiny and the leader. In: L. Spears (Ed.). *Insights on Leadership: Service, Stewardship, Spirit, and Servant-Leadership.* New York: John Wiley & Sons, pp. 258–270.

Jaworski, J. (1996). *Synchronicity: The Inner Path of Leadership.* San Francisco: Berret-Koehler Publishers.

Jeffries, E. (1998). Work as a calling. In: L. Spears (Ed.). *Insights on Leadership: Service, Stewardship, Spirit, and Servant-Leadership,* New York: John Wiley & Sons, pp. 29–37.

Jelinek, M. (1979). *Institutionalizing Innovation: A Study of Organizational Learning Systems.* New York: Praeger.

Jick, T. (1993). Implementing change. In: T. Jick (Ed.). *Managing Change.* Homewood, IL: Irwin, pp. 192–201.

Jones, M. (1995). *Creating an Imaginative Life.* Berkley: Conari Press.

Kanter, R., Stein, B., and Jick, T. (1992). *The Challenge of Organizational Change,* New York: Free Press.

Katz, R. (Spring 1997). Higher Education and the forces of self-organization: An interview with Margaret Wheatley. *Cause/Effect* **20** (1), pp. 18–21.

Kelly, K. (1994). *Out of Control: The New Biology of Machines, Social Systems, and the Economic World.* Reading, MA: Addison-Wesley.

Kets de Vries, M.R.F. and Miller, S. (1987). *Unstable at the Top: Inside the Troubled Organization.* New York: New American Library Books.

Kets de Vries, M.R.F. and Associates. (1991). *Organizations on the Couch: Clinical Perspectives on Organizational Behaviour and Change.* San Francisco: Jossey-Bass.

Kleiner, A. (1996). *The Age of Heretics: Heroes, Outlaws and the Forerunners of Corporate Change,* New York: Currency Doubleday.

Kolb, D. (1984). *Experiential Learning.* Englewood Cliffs, NJ: Prentice-Hall.

Kornfield, J. and Feldman, C. (Eds.). (1996). *Soul Food, Stories to Nourish the Spirit and the Heart.* San Francisco: Harper.

Kotter, J. P. (May–June 1990). What leaders really do. *Harvard Business Review,* pp. 103–111.

Kotter, J. and Schlesinger, L. (1987). *The Leadership Challenge: How to get Extraordinary Things done in Organizations.* San Francisco: Jossey-Bass.

Kouzes, J.M. and Posner, B.Z. (1995). *The Leadership Challenge: How to Keep Getting Extraordinary Things Done in Organizations.* San Francisco: Jossey-Bass.

Langley, A. (1991). Formal analysis and strategic decision-making. *Omega* **19** (213), pp. 79–99.

Leider, R.J. and Shapiro, D.A. (1995). *Repacking Your Bags.* San Francisco: Berret-Koehler Publishers.

Lessem, R. (1996). *From Hunter to Rainmaker: The Southern African Businessphere.* Randburg: Knowledge Resources.

Levitt, B. and March, J.G. (1988). Organizational Learning. *Annual Review of Sociology* 14, pp. 319–340.

Levy, D. (Summer 1994). Chaos theory and strategy: Theory, application and managerial implications. *Strategic Management Journal* (15), pp. 167–178.

Lewin, R. and Regine, B. (1999). *The Soul at Work: Unleashing the Power of Complexity Science for Business Success.* London: Orion Publishing Group.

London, S. (1997). *The New Science of Leadership: An Interview with Margaret Wheatley.* Radio Series: Insight & Outlook. URL: http://www.west.net/~insight/, pp. 1–6.

Mandela, N.R. (1996). *A Long Walk to Freedom.* London: Abacus.

Manz, C.C. and Sims, H.P. (Jr.). (1993). Superleadership: Leading others to lead themselves. In: J.L. Pierce and J.W. Newstrom (Eds.). *The Manager's Bookshelf: A Mosaic of Contemporary Views* (3 ed.). New York: HarperCollins College Publishers, pp. 139–148.

Marris, P. (1974). *Loss and Change.* IRoutledge & Kegan Paul.

Marsick, V.J. (1990). Action learning and reflection in the workplace. In: J.D. Mezirow (Ed.). *Fostering Critical Reflection in Adulthood.* San Francisco: Jossey-Bass.

Martin, I. (1997). *The Cardiovascular Disease Epidemics: A New Global Challenge for WHO.* URL address: http//www.healtnet.org/programs/procor/983comm.html.

McClelland, D.C. (July–August 1962). Business drive and national achievement. *Harvard Business Review* 40, pp. 99–112.

McClelland, D.C. and Burnham, D.H. (March–April 1976). Power is the great motivation. *Harvard Business Review* 54, pp. 100–110.

McCollum, J. (1995). Chaos, complexity, and servant-leadership. In: L. Spears (Ed.). *Reflections on Leadership: How Robert Greenleaf's Theory of Servant-leadership Influenced Today's Top Management Thinkers.* New York: John Wiley & Sons.

McGregor, D. (1960). *The Human Side of Enterprise.* New York: McGraw-Hill.

Meadows, D.H., Meadows, D.L., Randers, J. and Behrens, W.W. III (1972). *The Limits to Growth: A Report for the Club Of Rome's Project on the Predicament of Mankind.* New York: Universe Books.

Melrose, K. (1996). Leader as servant. *Executive Excellence* **13** (4), p. 20.

Menzies Lyth, I. (1988). Containing anxiety in organizations. *Selected Essays* I, London: Tavistock Institute.

Merry, U. (1995). *Coping with Uncertainty: Insights from the New Sciences of Chaos, Self-Organization, and Complexity.* Praeger.

Mezirow, J.D. (1990). How critical reflection triggers transformative learning. In: J.D. Mezirow, (Ed.). *Fostering Critical Reflection in Adulthood*. San Francisco: Jossey-Bass.

Mindell, A. (1992). *The Leader as Martial Artist*. San Francisco: HarperCollins.

Mintzberg, H. (January–February 1994). The fall and rise of strategic planning. *Harvard Business Review*, pp. 107–114.

Mintzberg, H. and Waters, J.A. (1990). Does decision get in the way. *Organizational Studies* **11** (1), pp. 1–5.

Morgan, G. (1988). *Riding the Waves of Change: Developing Managerial Competencies for a Turbulent World*. San Francisco: Jossey-Bass.

Morgan, G. (1986). *Images of Organization*. San Francisco: Jossey-Bass.

MTN Corporate Survey (1999). The knowledge pioneers. *Knowledge Management* **1** (3), pp. 59–74.

Nadler, D. (1983). *Concepts for the Management of Organization Change*. Section V Organization, Adaptation and Change. Delta Consulting Group.

Naidoo, P. (1998). *A Fractal Image of Leadership*. (Working paper, Graduate School of Business, University of Cape Town).

Nasser, M.E. and Vivier, F.J. (1993). *Mindset for the New Generation Organization*. Kenwyn: Juta.

Nel, C. (1994). Value-centred leadership: The journey to becoming a world-class organization. In: P. Christie, R. Lessem and L. Mbigi (Eds.). *African Management: Philosophies, Concepts and Applications*. Cape Town: Knowledge Resources.

Nonaka, I. And Takeuchi, H. (1995). *The Knowledge-Creating Company*. New York: Oxford University Press.

Nonaka, I. (November–December 1991). The knowledge-creating company. *Harvard Business Review*, pp. 96–104.

Norgaard, M. (October 1996). Toward transformation. *Executive Excellence* **13** (10), p. 20.

Novak, M. (1996). *Business as a Calling: Work and the Examined Life*. New York: Free Press.

Nystrom, P.C. and Starbuck, W. (1984). To avoid organizational crises, unlearn. *Organizational Dynamics* 13, pp. 53–65.

Pascale, R.T. (Summary prepared by Stephen Rubenfeld) (1993). Managing on the edge: How successful companies use conflict to stay ahead. In: J.L. Pierce and J.W. Newstrom (Eds.). *The Manager's Bookshelf: A Mosaic of Contemporary Views* (3 ed.). New York: HarperCollins College Publishers., pp. 289–293.

Pascale, R.T. (1990). *Managing on the Edge: How Successful Companies Use Conflict to Stay Ahead*. London: Viking Penguin.

Pearson, C.S. (1989). *The Hero Within: Six Archetypes We Live By*. New York: Harper & Row.

Peat, F.D. (1994). *Lighting the Seventh Fire: The Spiritual Ways, Healing, and Science of the Native American*. New York: Birch Lane Press.

Peters, T. (1994a). *The Pursuit of WOW!: Every Person's Guide to Topsy-Turvy Times*. New York: Vintage Books.

Peters, T. (1994b). *The Tom Peters Seminar: Crazy Times Call for Crazy Organizations*. New York: Vintage Books.

Peters, T.J. and Waterman, R.H. (1982). *In Search of Excellence*. New York: Harper & Row.

Pinkola Estes, C. (1992). *Women Who Run With the Wolves: Myths and Stories of the Wild Woman Archetype*. New York: Ballantine Books.

Poole, M. S. and DeSanctis, G. (1990). Understanding the use of group decision support systems: The theory of adaptive structuration. In: J. Fulk and C. Steinfield (Eds.). *Organizations and Communication Technology*, Newbury Park, CA: Sage, pp. 173–191.

Porter, M. (November–December 1996). What is strategy? *Harvard Business Review*, pp. 61–78.

Powell, T.C. and Dent-Micallef, A. (1997). Information technology as competitive advantage: The role of human, business, and technology resources. *Strategic Management Journal* **18** (5), pp. 375–405.

Prigogine, J. and Stengers, I. (1984). *Order out of Chaos: Man's New Dialogue with Nature*. New York: Bantam.

Quigley, M.E. (May 1997). Quantum organizations. *Executive Excellence* **14** (5), pp. 14–15.

Ramsay, S.M. (1994). Leading with art and soul. *Executive Excellence* **11** (12), pp. 18–19.

Reina, D.S. and Reina, M.L. (1999). *Trust and Betrayal in the Workplace: Building Effective Relationships in Your Organization*. San Francisco: Berret-Koehler Publishers.

Revans, R.W. (1998). *The ABC of Action Learning*. London: Lemos and Crane.

Revans, R.W. (1982). *The Origins and Growth of Action Learning*. Bickley: Chartwell-Bratt.

Revans, R.W. (1978). *The ABC of Action Learning: A Review of 25 Years of Experience*. Luton: Action Learning Trust.

Rigano, D. and Edwards, J. (1998). 'Incorporating reflection into work practice: A case study. *Management Learning* **29** (4), pp. 431–446.

Roberts, C. and Kleiner, A. (1999). Five kinds of systems thinking. In: P. Senge, A. Kleiner, C. Roberts, R. Ross and G. Roth (Eds.). *The Dance of Change: The Challenges of Sustaining Momentum in Learning Organisations*. London: Nicholas Brealey Publishing, pp. 137–149

Robbins, P.R. (1997). *Managing Today!* Englewood Cliffs, NJ: Prentice-Hall.

Rockefeller, J.D. (1973). *The Second American Revolution.* New York: Harper-Row, pp. 72.

Sadler, P. (1997). *Leadership: Styles — Role Models — Qualities — Behaviours,* London: Kogan Page.

Sams, J. and Carson, D. (1988). *Medicine Cards: The Discovery of Power Through the Way of Animals.* Sante Fé: Bear & Company.

Saunders, E. (February 1998). Leadership the South African way. *People Dynamics,* pp. 31–34.

Schein, E. (1987). *The Clinical Perspective in Fieldwork.* Newbury, CA: Sage Publications.

Schön, D. (1983). *The Reflective Practitioner.* New York: Basic Books.

Schutz, W. (1994). *The Human Element: Productivity, Self-Esteem and the Bottom Line,* San Francisco: Jossey-Bass.

Senge, P. (1996). Rethinking leadership in the learning organization. *The Systems Thinker* **7** (1), pp. 1–8.

Senge, P. (August 1995a). Making a better world. *Executive Excellence,* pp. 18–19.

Senge, P. (1995b). Robert Greenleaf's legacy: A new foundation for twenty-first century institutions. In: L. Spears (Ed.). *Reflections on Leadership: How Robert K. Greenleaf's Theory of Servant-leadership Influenced Today's Top Management Thinkers.* New York: John Wiley & Sons.

Senge, P. (1994). *The Fifth Discipline Fieldbook.* London: Nicholas Brealey Publishing.

Senge, P. (1990a). *The Fifth Discipline: The Art & Practice of the Learning Organization.* New York: Doubleday Currency.

Senge, P. (Fall 1990b). The leader's new work: Building learning organizations. *Sloan Management Review,* pp. 7–23.

Senge, P., Kleiner, R., Roberts, C., Ross, R. and Roth, G. (1999). *The Dance of Change: The Challenge of Sustaining Momentum in Learning Organizations.* London: Nicholas Brealey Publishing.

Senge, P., Kleiner, R., Roberts, C., Ross, R. and Smith, B. (1995). *The Fifth Discipline Fieldbook: Strategies and Tools for Building a Learning Organization.* London: Nicholas Brealey Publishing.

Shrivastava, P. (1983). A typology of organizational learning systems. *Journal of Management Studies* **20**, pp. 1–28.

Siegel, B. (1996). Love: The work of the soul. In: R. Carlson and B. Shields (Eds.). *Handbook for the Soul.* Great Britain: Piatkus.

Silver, W. (1993). *Metacognitive Leadership: An Integrative Approach to Leadership Education and Development.* (Presentation at the Organization Behavior Teaching Conference, Bucknell University, PA).

Spangler, D. (1996). *A Pilgrim in Aquarius.* Findhorn Press, Forres.

Spears, L.C. (Ed.) (1998). *Insights on Leadership: Service, Stewardship, Spirit, and Servant-Leadership.* New York: John Wiley & Sons.

Spears, L. (Ed.) (1995). *Reflections on Leadership: How Robert K. Greenleaf's Theory of Servant Leadership Influenced Today's Top Management Thinkers.* New York: John Wiley & Sons.

Spencer, L.J. (1989). *Winning Through Participation.* Dubuque: Kendall/Hunt Publishing Company.

Stacey, R. (1996). *Strategic Management and Organizational Dynamics* (2 ed.). London: Pitman Publishing.

Stacey, R. (1995). The science of complexity. *Strategic Management Journal* **16**, pp. 477–495.

Stacey, R. (1992). *Managing Chaos: Dynamic Business Strategies in an Unpredictable World,* London: Saxon Printing.

Stacey, R. (1991). *The Chaos Frontier: Creative Strategic Control for Business.* Oxford: Butterworth-Heinemann.

Starbuck, W. and Hedberg, B. (1977). Saving an organization from a stagnating environment. In: H. Thorelli (Ed.). *Strategy + Structure = Performance.* Bloomington, IN: Indiana University Press, pp. 133–148.

Stata, R. (Spring 1989). Organizational learning — The key to management innovation. *Sloan Management Review,* pp. 63–74.

Storr, A. (1983). *The Essential Jung.* New York: MJF Books.

Strebel, P. (May–June 1996). Why do employees resist change. *Harvard Business Review* **17** (1), pp. 27–31.

Tice, L. (April 1996). Leader as mentor. *Executive Excellence,* pp. 19.

Tichy, N.M. and Devanna, M.A. (1986). *The Transformational Leader.* New York: Wiley.

Tidhult, I. (1997). *How can Complexity Theory help us Navigate the Future — A Dynamic Perspective?* (Lecture Series Summaries, Skandia Future Center, pp. 1–7).

Townsend, P.L. and Gebhardt, J.E. (1997). Active followership. *Executive Excellence* **14** (4), pp. 10.

Toynbee, A. (1992). *Change and Habit: The Challenge of Our Time (Global Thinkers).* New York: Oxford University Press.

Tregoe, B.B., Zimmerman, J.W., Smith, R.A. and Tobia, P.M. (1990). *Vision in Action: How to Integrate your Company's Strategic Goals into Day-to-Day Management Decisions.* New York: Fireside.

Van der Merwe, L. (1994). A learning community with a common purpose. In: P. Christie, R. Lessem and L. Mbigi (Eds.). *African Management: Philosophies, Concepts and Applications,* Cape Town: Knowledge Resources.

Van der Post, L. (1995). *The Dark Eye of Africa.* London: The Hogarth Press, p. 124.

Vint, A., Recaldin, C. and Gould, D. (1998). *Learning to Fly: Leadership & Performance in the Boardroom*, London: Kogan.

Walsch, N.D. (1997). *Conversations With God, An Uncommon Dialogue.* Hodder & Stoughton.

Watkins, E.J and Marsick, V.J (1993). *Sculpting the Learning Organization. Lessons in the Art and Science of Systematic Change.* San Fransisco: Jossey-Bass.

Weisbord, M.R. and Janoff, S. (1995). *Future Search: An Action Guide to Finding Common Ground in Organizations and Communities*, San Francisco: Berret-Koehler Publishers.

Welch, J. (1996). *General Electric Annual Report.* Stamford, CT.

Wheatley, M.J. (1999). *Leadership and the New Science: Discovering Order in a Chaotic World* (2 ed.). San Francisco: Berret-Koehler Publishers.

Wheatley, M.J. (1998). What is our work? In: L. Spears (Ed.). *Insights on Leadership: Service, Stewardship, Spirit, and Servant-Leadership.* New York: John Wiley & Sons, pp. 340–351.

Wheatley, M.J. (1992). *Leadership and the New Science: Learning about Organization from an Orderly Universe.* San Franscisco: Berret-Koehler Publishers.

Wheatley, M.J. and Kellner-Rogers, M. (1996). *A Simpler Way.* San Franscisco: Berret-Koehler Publishers.

White, R.P, Hodgson, P. and Crainer, S. (1996). *The Future of Leadership: Riding the Corporate Rapids into the 21st Century.* Maryland: Pitman Publishing.

Whittington, R. (1993). *What is Strategy — and Does It Matter?* London: International Thomson Business Press.

Whyte, D. (1994). *The Heart Aroused: Poetry and the Preservation of the Soul in Corporate America.* New York: Currency Doubleday.

Wild, H., Bishop, L. and Sullivan, C.L. (1996). *Building Environments for Learning and Innovation.* Institute for Research on Learning.

Willcocks, S.G. and Rees, C.J. (1995). A psychoanalytic perspective on organizational change. *Leadership & Organization Development Journal* **16** (5), pp. 32–37.

World Health Organization. (1998). *The World Health Report 1998: Life in the 21st Century — A Vision for All.* Geneva: WHO.

Zaleznik, A. (March–April 1992). Managers and leaders: Are they different? *Harvard Business Review*, pp. 126–235.

Zohar, D. (1997). *Rewiring the Corporate Brain: Using New Science to rethink How We Structure and Lead Organizations.* San Francisco: Berret-Koehler Publishers.

Zohar, D. and Marshall, I. (2000). *SQ: Spiritual Intelligence — The Ultimate Intelligence.* London: Bloomsbury Publishing.